THE GREEK TRAGEDY
IN NEW TRANSLATIONS

GENERAL EDITORS
Peter Burian and Alan Shapiro

EURIPIDES: Bakkhai

EURIPIDES

Bakkhai

Translated by
REGINALD GIBBONS
With Introduction and Notes by
CHARLES SEGAL

OXFORD
UNIVERSITY PRESS

2001

OXFORD

UNIVERSITY PRESS

Oxford New York
Athens Auckland Bangkok Bogotá Buenos Aires Calcutta
Cape Town Chennai Dar es Salaam Delhi Florence Hong Kong Istanbul
Karachi Kuala Lumpur Madrid Melbourne Mexico City Mumbai
Nairobi Paris São Paulo Shanghai Singapore Taipei Tokyo Toronto Warsaw

and associated companies in
Berlin Ibadan

Copyright © 2001 by Oxford University Press, Inc.

Published by Oxford University Press, Inc.
198 Madison Avenue, New York, New York 10016

Library of Congress Cataloging-in-Publication Data
Euripides.
[Bacchae. English]
Bakkhai / Euripides; translated by Reginald Gibbons; with an introduction
and notes by Charles Segal.
p. cm. — (The Greek tragedy in new translations)
ISBN 0-19-512598-3
1. Pentheus (Greek mythology)—Drama. 2. Dionysus (Greek deity)—Drama. 3. Bac-
chantes—Drama. I. Gibbons, Reginald. II. Segal, Charles, 1936– III. Title.
IV. Series.
PA3975.B2 G53 2000
882'.01—dc21   00-020180

9 8 7 6 5 4 3 2 1
Printed in the United States of America

EDITORS' FOREWORD

"The Greek Tragedy in New Translations is based on the conviction that poets like Aeschylus, Sophocles, and Euripides can only be properly rendered by translators who are themselves poets. Scholars may, it is true, produce useful and perceptive versions. But our most urgent present need is for a *re-creation* of these plays—as though they had been written, freshly and greatly, by masters fully at home in the English of our own times."

With these words, the late William Arrowsmith announced the purpose of this series, and we intend to honor that purpose. As was true of most of the volumes that began to appear in the 1970s—first under Arrowsmith's editorship, later in association with Herbert Golder— those for which we bear editorial responsibility are products of close collaboration between poets and scholars. We believe (as Arrowsmith did) that the skills of both are required for the difficult and delicate task of transplanting these magnificent specimens of another culture into the soil of our own place and time, to do justice both to their deep differences from our patterns of thought and expression and to their palpable closeness to our most intimate concerns. Above all, we are eager to offer contemporary readers dramatic poems that convey as vividly and directly as possible the splendor of language, the complexity of image and idea, and the intensity of emotion of the originals. This entails, among much else, the recognition that the tragedies were meant for performance—as scripts for actors—to be sung and danced as well as spoken. It demands writing of inventiveness, clarity, musicality, and dramatic power. By such standards we ask that these translations be judged.

This series is also distinguished by its recognition of the need of nonspecialist readers for a critical introduction informed by the best recent scholarship, but written clearly and without condescension.

Each play is followed by notes designed not only to elucidate obscure references but also to mediate the conventions of the Athenian stage as well as those features of the Greek text that might otherwise go unnoticed. The notes are supplemented by a glossary of mythical and geographical terms that should make it possible to read the play without turning elsewhere for basic information. Stage directions are sufficiently ample to aid readers in imagining the action as they read. Our fondest hope, of course, is that these versions will be staged not only in the minds of their readers but also in the theaters to which, after so many centuries, they still belong.

A NOTE ON THE SERIES FORMAT

A series such as this requires a consistent format. Different translators, with individual voices and approaches to the material in hand, cannot be expected to develop a single coherent style for each of the three tragedians, much less make clear to modern readers that, despite the differences among the tragedians themselves, the plays share many conventions and a generic, or period, style. But they can at least share a common format and provide similar forms of guidance to the reader.

1. Spelling of Greek names

Orthography is one area of difference among the translations that requires a brief explanation. Historically, it has been the common practice to use Latinized forms of Greek names when bringing them into English. Thus, for example, Oedipus (not Oidipous) and Clytemnestra (not Klutaimestra) are customary in English. Recently, however, many translators have moved toward more precise transliteration, which has the advantage of presenting the names as both Greek and new, instead of Roman and neoclassical importations into English. In the case of so familiar a name as Oedipus, however, transliteration risks the appearance of pedantry or affectation. And in any case, perfect consistency cannot be expected in such matters. Readers will feel the same discomfort with "Athenai" as the chief city of Greece as they would with "Platon" as the author of the *Republic*.

The earlier volumes in this series adopted as a rule a "mixed" orthography in accordance with the considerations outlined above. The most familiar names retain their Latinate forms, the rest are transliterated; –os rather than Latin—*us* is adopted for the termination of masculine names, and Greek diphthongs (such as Iphigen*ei*a for Latin Iphigenia) are retained. Some of the later volumes continue this practice, but where translators have preferred to use a more consistent practice of transliteration or Latinization, we have honored their wishes.

2. Stage directions

The ancient manuscripts of the Greek plays do not supply stage directions (though the ancient commentators often provide information relevant to staging, delivery, "blocking," etc.). Hence stage directions must be inferred from words and situations and our knowledge of Greek theatrical conventions. At best this is a ticklish and uncertain procedure. But it is surely preferable that good stage directions should be provided by the translator than that readers should be left to their own devices in visualizing action, gesture, and spectacle. Ancient tragedy was austere and "distanced" by means of masks, which means that the reader must not expect the detailed intimacy ("He shrugs and turns wearily away," "She speaks with deliberate slowness, as though to emphasize the point," etc.) that characterizes stage directions in modern naturalistic drama.

3. Numbering of lines

For the convenience of the reader who may wish to check the English against the Greek text or vice versa, the lines have been numbered according to both the Greek text and the translation. The lines of the English translation have been numbered in multiples of ten, and these numbers have been set in the right-hand margin. The notes that follow the text have been keyed to the line numbers of the translation. The (inclusive) Greek numeration will be found bracketed at the top of the page. Readers will doubtless note that in many plays the English lines outnumber the Greek, but they should not therefore conclude that the translator has been unduly prolix. In most cases the reason is simply that the translator has adopted the free-flowing norms of modern Anglo-American prosody, with its brief-breath- and emphasis-determined lines, and its habit of indicating cadence and caesuras by line length and setting rather than by conventional punctuation. Other translators have preferred to cast dialogue in more regular five-beat or six-beat lines, and in these cases Greek and English numerations will tend to converge.

Durham, N.C.   PETER BURIAN
Chapel Hill, N.C.   ALAN SHAPIRO
2000

CONTENTS

BAKKHAI

INTRODUCTION

DIONYSOS

Dionysos is the god of Letting Go. One of his cult titles repeatedly alluded to in the *Bakkhai* is Lysios, the Releaser. He liberates from the constrictions and restraints of ordinary social life. He does this through his gifts of wine, his breakdown of inhibitions in group ecstasy and excited dancing and singing, and through the lesser intoxications of the illusion-inducing power of the mask and the theater. He offers a liberating surrender of self that, in the extreme and nightmarish form envisaged in the play, brings homicidal madness. In its more benign version however, it offers the restorative blessings of festivity, collective enjoyment, and the exhilarating release of barriers between oneself and others. Letting go, surrendering control, yielding to the intoxicating effects of wine or exciting music, total fusion with the group in emotional participation and exultation in our animal energies—these are the gifts that Dionysos holds out to Thebes and through Thebes to all of Greece, that is (in our terms), to the civilized world.

The king of Thebes, Pentheus, is repelled by this new cult, but he is also increasingly fascinated and drawn in. For him, as for us (and perhaps for many in the original audience), Dionysiac worship is both thrilling and dangerous. On a psychological reading (and this has been a traditional way of approaching the play), Dionysos fundamentally challenges Pentheus' view of what he is and thus opens up an identity crisis that ends in disintegration, both emotional and physical. In their first face-to-face encounter, Pentheus is blind to the numinous power in the Stranger's presence (587), "Where is he, then? My eyes don't see him here." The Stranger makes a direct assault on his identity (592): "You don't know what your life is, nor what you're doing, nor who you are."

Tragic drama involves us in the lives and feelings of individuals; and here we have no trouble in responding to the antagonisms of the *Bak-khai*. Pentheus, king of Thebes, and Dionysos, the new god just arrived from Asia Minor, are both doubles and opposites. They are in fact cousins (Semelé, Dionysos' mother, is the sister of Agauë, Pentheus' mother); both are young; both, in very different ways, are inexorably determined to establish their place and authority in their city. Pentheus, ruler of the heavily walled, seven-gated city of Thebes, is concerned, if not obsessed, with law and order and with his martial authority. Dionysos, who appears in the play disguised as the handsome Stranger from Lydia, arrives with a band of exotically dressed women devotees who praise the new god's blessings of wine and song to the accompaniment of foreign-sounding flutes and drums. It is as if a group of outlandishly dressed Hare Krishnas perform their dances in front of an orderly Midwestern City Hall. Or one might compare Pentheus' crackdown on the maenads with modern authorities' response to the drug culture—except that for Euripides' contemporaries Dionysos is already an established god and has a firm place in their religious and civic life.

The psychological conflicts are involving, but much more is at stake. What we might read as the language of the self is also the language of religious revelation, the announcement of the mysteries and the rites of which the new god is the center.[1] Dionysos' arrival also raises the question of the balance between restraint and release in a healthy social order. Just fifty years before the *Bakkhai*, the Furies of Aeschylus' *Eumenides* declared (528–30): "Neither a life of anarchy /nor a life under a despot / should you praise. / To all that lies in the middle has a god given excellence."[2] And soon afterwards Athena herself, patron goddess of Athens, endorsed these principles in the reconciliation that gives the dread goddesses a firm place in her city (690–700): "In this place shall the awe / of the citizens and their inborn dread restrain / injustice, both day and night alike, / so long as the citizens themselves do not pervert the laws / by evil influxes . . . / Neither anarchy nor tyranny shall the citizens defend and respect, if they follow my counsel; / and they shall not cast out altogether from the city what is to be feared. / For who among mortals that fears nothing is just? / Such is the object of awe that you must justly dread . . ." The mood in Athens at the time of the *Bakkhai* is very different, and yet the issues are similar. Once more a strange and potent divinity is at the city gates, and the city must

---

1. See my essay, "Euripides' *Bacchae*: The Language of the Self and the Language of the Mysteries," in my *Interpreting Greek Tragedy: Myth, Poetry, Text.* (Ithaca, 1986), 294–312.

2. This and the following translation from the *Eumenides* are from Hugh Lloyd-Jones, trans., *Aeschylus: Oresteia: Eumenides* (Englewood Cliffs, N.J., 1970).

find the safe and proper way of accepting or rejecting him. Aeschylus' Athens could find a mode of accommodation with those awesome powers in accordance with its civic and religious institutions. In the *Bakkhai* the Theban ruler would resist to the death, barricade the city, and lock up the intruders.[3] But the divine intruder here is not a dread, quasi-monstrous underworld power but a pleasure-giving, laughing god with long blond hair and the flush of wine on his face. Yet just this allure in the god's outward appearance makes him all the more insidious to Pentheus.

What is it about Dionysos and his gifts that makes us hesitant to accept them or suspicious of the benefits they bring? Why should Culture resist the impulses to pleasure and the free play of animal instincts to which the god beckons? Why should we not simply welcome a god who offers us joy in our kinship with nature and delight in spontaneous emotional and physical expression? These questions become most acute when we are face to face with the gifts that Dionysos offers, hear the exciting music of his worshipers, and are drawn to leap with pounding feet into the Dionysiac dance and join in the shouts of *euhoi* with the ecstatic dancers. It is at this point, when Dionysos actually begins to transform our being, that resistance arises. This is the point at which the stage action of the *Bakkhai* begins, with the dancing of the god's initiates and the arrival of the god himself, in the guise of the luxurious Stranger, the Eastern Barbarian, the Other—beautiful and seductive but also in some way terrifying.

Whether the play means us to identify with the triumph of the god or with the cost to his human antagonists remains the basic interpretive question. Euripides' presentation of the gods is never simple, and interpreters continue to be divided between a Euripides who defends the religious tradition and a Euripides who criticizes it.[4] Euripides wrote his play, I believe, in a way that allows his audience to experience the conflicting responses that Dionysos can arouse. In my view Euripides

---

3. On the different modes of Athenian and Theban response to such outsiders see Froma I. Zeitlin, "Thebes: Theater of Self and Society in Athenian Drama," in John J. Winkler and F. I. Zeitlin, eds., *Nothing to Do with Dionysus?* (Princeton, 1990), 130–67; also her "Staging Dionysos between Thebes and Athens," in Thomas H. Carpenter and Christopher A. Faraone, eds., *Masks of Dionysus* (Itheca, N.Y., 1993), 147–82.

4. To take a recent example of extreme positions, for Seaford the play is essentially a celebration of Dionysos' positive, unifying role in the polis (Richard Seaford, ed. and trans., *Euripides, Bacchae* [Warminster, 1996], 46–51; also his *Reciprocity and Ritual* [Oxford, 1994], 255–56, 293–327), whereas for Stephen Esposito, ed. and trans., *The Bacchae of Euripides* (Newburyport, Mass., 1998), 1, "Euripides' *Bacchae* is arguably the darkest and most ferocious tragedy ever written." For the diversity of recent opinion see C. Segal, *Dionysiac Poetics and Euripides' Bacchae*, 2nd ed. (Princeton, 1997), Afterword, 349–93, also Paul Woodruff, ed. and trans., *Euripides, Bacchae* (Indianapolis, 1998), xxix–xxxviii.

is neither attacking nor defending Dionysos, any more than he is celebrating some sort of conversion from his previous skepticism about the Olympian religion. Rather, he examines the problematical aspects of the cult, reveals both its beauty and its horror, and thereby explores the phenomena of collective violence and madness in ways that reach beyond the play's historical and religious moment.

DIONYSOS AND THE BAKKHAI

Three and half centuries after its first official performance in Athens in 405 B.C.E., the Bakkhai figures in what is surely the most bizarre moment of literary reception in the annals of theater. In 53 B.C.E. the victorious Parthian commander brought the head of the defeated Roman general, Crassus, killed in battle, to a feast at the Parthian court. A Greek tragic actor who was present as part of the entertainment — one Jason of Tralles — seized the head and recited lines 1324–26 of the Bakkhai, the horrific moment when the still mad Agauë enters carrying the severed head of her son, Pentheus: ". . . from the mountain, / And for this house, we bring in a blessèd hunt, / A fresh-cut tendril." The performance delighted the audience, Plutarch reports, and Jason received a huge reward from the Parthian king (Life of Crassus 33).

There are fascinating coincidences of this event with the original creation and perhaps trial performance of the Bakkhai at the court of King Archelaus of Macedon in the last decade of the fifth century B.C.E. A play written at the northern fringes of the Greek world about the encounter of Greek and non-Greek ("barbarian") cultures is reenacted centuries later (albeit partially) in an even more remote setting and with myth transmuted to life — with an even more perplexing mixture of beauty and savagery and an even sharper clash of cultures. Plutarch implies two contradictory audience responses, that of the delighted Parthians who, as Plutarch describes the scene, enter into the performance with gusto, and that of his own intended audience of cultivated Greeks (and perhaps Romans) in a more stable and, on the whole, more peaceful world, with which we can easily identify two millennia later. This contradictory mixture of pleasure and horror in audience response is prophetic of the play's reception and imitation from antiquity to today; and what Gilbert Norwood called "The Riddle of the Bakkhai" (Manchester, 1908) continues to puzzle, disturb, and provoke.

Exactly why, in the last years of his long life (ca. 480–406 B.C.E.), Euripides left Athens for Macedon we do not know. He may have been lured by Archelaus' ambitious cultural program, which attracted poets and musicians from the entire Greek world. Living in Macedon, in any case, Euripides may have had a more intense experience of the collective and individual emotions stirred by the Dionysiac rituals that are at the center of the *Bakkhai*. The women of that region, Plutarch reports in his *Life of Alexander the Great*, were especially given to orgiastic rites in Dionysiac-Orphic bands, or *thiasoi* (sg. *thiasos*), that practiced ecstasy, possession, and snake handling.[5] Yet plays on Dionysiac themes had been a part of the tragic repertoire; and most of the attributes of Dionysos in the *Bakkhai* were familiar to Athenians, whether in cult, myth, or art. The play won first prize when it was performed in Athens shortly after the poet's death.[6]

Ambiguity seems to be an essential part of Euripides' conception of Dionysos. The god is "[m]ost terrible to mortals and most gentle," as he himself (in disguise) states at a climactic moment (980). Like other gods of Greek tragedy—one thinks especially of the Aphrodite of Euripides' *Hippolytos*—Dionysos exacts terrible punishment for slights to his divinity; and, as in the case of Aphrodite, that punishment takes the form of an exaggerated and destructive enactment of the god's gifts, here the deadly initiation of Pentheus and the murderous ecstasy of the Theban maenads.

Euripides' audience would have other points of reference for this mixture of beauty and fearfulness in the god: Dionysiac myths of both male and female violence against kin, tales about the god's miracles on his arrival at new places, ominous stories about the invention of wine, initiation ceremonies, descents to the underworld, citywide rituals of masking and dressing as satyrs, processions in which phallic images are carried by young girls, fertility rites, sacred marriages, and above all festive times when the new wine is opened and tasted. In contrast to what the play itself might suggest, Dionysos' widespread and popular festivals generally have happy associations in Greek religion and are characterized by an atmosphere of license, freedom, and good cheer. We have little experience of such public, religiously sanctioned suspension of normal restraints on social behavior. Our closest analo-

5. Plutarch, *Life of Alexander*, c. 2. The references to northern Greece and to the rivers of Macedonia (*Bakkhai* 409–15, 568–75) are indications of the play's composition there.
6. See Thomas H. Carpenter, *Dionysiac Imagery in Fifth-Century Athens* (Oxford, 1997), 117–18. For an excellent overview of Dionysos, with abundant bibliography, see Albert Henrichs, "Dionysos," in Simon Hornblower and Anthony Spawforth, eds., *Oxford Classical Dictionary*, 3rd ed. (Oxford, 1996), 479–82; idem, " 'He Has a God in Him': Human and Divine in the Modern Perception of Dionysos," in Carpenter and Faraone, eds., *Masks of Dionysus*, 13–43; also Walter Burkert, *Greek Religion*, trans. John Raffan (Cambridge, Mass., 1985), 161–67, 237–42; Carlo Gasparri, et al., "Dionysos," "Dionysos/Fufluns," "Dionysos/Bacchus," etc., in *Lexicon Iconographiae Mythologiae Classicae* (Zurich and Munich, 1986), vol. 3, part 1, pp. 414–566; vol. 3, part 2, pp. 296–456 (plates). For further bibliography see my *Dionysiac Poetics*, 405–11.

gies are perhaps Halloween or the carnival festivals that survive here and there. Mob excitement turning from exhilaration to violence at rock concerts or soccer matches and the like provides some secular parallels, and the intervention of the police on these occasions indicates the threat that society feels in such outbursts.

As Dionysos tells us in his opening lines, he is the son of Zeus but also the child of a mortal mother, the Theban Semelé, the daughter of Kadmos and aunt of Pentheus. This collocation of divinity and mortality also reflects his paradoxical combination of Olympian status and closeness to the earth as a divinity of fertility and liquid energy. He can claim native Greek origins; but, in the guise of a handsome Lydian youth, he leads a band of female Dionysiac worshipers from Asia Minor. In fact, the Greeks of the archaic and classical periods generally imagine Dionysos as a foreign latecomer from Thrace or the East (where he may well have his earliest origins). As a new god, he is sensitive about his prerogatives and zealous to command the appropriate respect. In fact, Dionysos seems to have been already established in Greece in the Bronze Age, for his name occurs on Linear B tablets in the Mycenaean archives of Pylos and Crete around 1250 B.C.E.

For the Greeks of all periods Dionysos is best known as the inventor of viticulture and the god of wine. Over two thousand archaic and classical vases depict him in this role, leading bands of satyrs and bacchants amid vines, clusters of grapes, and entangling ivy. These trappings of his worship express the access to the untrammeled energies of wild nature that he offers to his followers. On the vases his bacchants wear the fawnskin, leap and dance energetically, handle snakes and other wild animals, and carry the thyrsos—a fennel stalk tipped with a cluster of ivy leaves. The accompanying satyrs, half-human and half-bestial, with pointed ears and horses' tails, enact an uninhibited release of animal energy with exuberant dancing, drunkenness, and a frank sexuality that still keeps these vases in storerooms.[7] This more frivolous spirit is reflected not only in the satyrs' imaginative antics in vase-painting but also in the comedies and satyr plays that were presented along with the tragedies at the Great or City Dionysia and the lesser Dionysiac festival, the Lenaea. In Aristophanes' *Frogs*, for instance, another play in which Dionysos is a main character, the god's ambiguous sexuality, unheroic demeanor, and fondness for wine, women, and song are a source of fun and laughter.

---

7. On the vases the god's female companions are probably nymphs rather than mortals: See Carpenter, *Dionysiac Imagery*, 52–69; Sarah Peirce, "Visual Language and Concepts of Cult in the 'Lenaia Vases,'" *Classical Antiquity* 17 (1998), 59–95, especially 54–67.

At Thebes and other cities (but not, apparently, at Athens) the female devotees of Dionysos went out on the mountain in an excited religious procession, known as the *oreibasia* (literally, mountain walking), of which the play gives an imaginative version in the two long messenger speeches. The combination of unsupervised women in forest or on mountain, a festive atmosphere, and wine was a scenario to excite suspicion, and Pentheus' response may not have been atypical. Euripides' *Ion* and fourth-century comedies make such festivals the setting for the sexual encounters that eventually produce the foundlings required by these plots.[8] More broadly, the stories and images associated with Dionysos may express the threats and the anxieties that the male-dominated society of fifth-century Athens feels toward the free expression of female emotion. It is symptomatic of this culture that women who are carried away by unrestrained feelings of joy, anger, or grief are described in Dionysiac imagery—and maenad means, literally, mad woman.[9] Agauë exemplifies the dangers of this Dionysiac emotion. In the insane ecstasy of the all-female band of worshipers, she tears apart her son like one of the animals shown on the vases (a ritual *sparagmos* or rending) and then exults over his body rather than lamenting over him, as women traditionally do in group threnodies in this society, and as she will in fact do when sanity returns.[10]

Happily, the gifts of Dionysos that dominate the two most popular festivals of the god at Athens are less complicated. At the Anthesteria the new wine is opened; at the Great Dionysia, where the *Bakkhai* was presented, there are phallic and other processions, choral song, and performances of tragedies and comedies. Both of these festivals have solemn moments, but the predominant mood is jollity, spontaneity, freedom from constraint, and exuberance. The odes of the first half of the *Bakkhai* reflect this spirit. An Attic red-figured vase of the latter half of the fifth century offers a remarkable parallel to the joyous atmosphere of the play's first stasimon, where Dionysos "[R]ejoices in festivities / And loves the goddess Peace—who gives us / Our plenty and

8. Pentheus reiterates his conviction that these maenadic rites are the occasions for illicit sex: see 260–77, 416–18, 541–45, 573, 793–95. For the lasciviousness in Dionysiac myth generally see Seaford, *Reciprocity*, 265–67.

9. See, e.g., Aeschylus, *Seven against Thebes* 835–36, *Suppliants* 562–64; Sophocles, *Trachinian Women* 216–20; Euripides, *Hecuba* 684–87 and 1075–78, *Phoenician Women* 1489–90. Bacchantic imagery also frequently describes violent and destructive male emotions, such as the fury of war or madness, as in Sophocles, *Antigone* 135–37 or Euripides, *Herakles* 889–93. See in general Renate Schlesier, "Mixtures of Masks: Maenads as Tragic Models," in Carpenter and Faraone, eds., *Masks of Dionysus*, 89–114, especially 98–114.

10. See *Bakkhai* 1323–55 and in general my *Dionysiac Poetics*, 362–66, with the further references there cited.

rears our children" (498–500). This vase depicts a youthful and sensual Dionysos surrounded by female figures who personify Peace, Grape Blossom, and Ripeness. They offer trays of fruit while a satyr quietly plays a lyre and another satyr, personifying Revel (Kômos), stands nearby. Hovering above Dionysos, a winged putto, symbolizing Desire, holds out a fillet.[11] Even this peaceful scene, however, shows the more unruly side of the god's gifts, for a satyr is about to attack one of the females.

At Athens, Dionysos also has important civic functions and is identified with the city's democratic spirit. He is a leveling god whose gifts are available to all and are celebrated in ways that blur the divisions of male and female, young and old, rich and poor, human and animal. His major festival, the Great Dionysia, expresses the strength, unity, and political concerns of the city.[12] This festival opened with a procession in which an ancient wooden statue of the god was carried from his shrine at Eleutherae, in the border territory near Thebes, to the god's precinct adjoining the theater, in the heart of the city, thereby symbolically linking the periphery of the city's territory with its center. Other events here, in the theater of Dionysos, have political and patriotic meaning: the libations by the ten elected generals, the display of the tribute paid by the subject allies of Athens' naval empire, and the parade of young men of military age whose fathers had been killed in battle and who were raised at state expense. (This is not to say that the plays presented at the festival necessarily endorse a political ideology or are propagandistic). At the Anthesteria Dionysos marries the wife of the King Archon, who has the ritual title of Basilinna, the Queen, in what may be a symbolical form of a Sacred Marriage (hieros gamos), promoting the well-being of the city through the union of god and mortal.

Throughout Attic tragedy Dionysos is invoked as a god of purification who can help the city at moments of crisis. In Sophocles' Antigone the troubled chorus calls upon him in these terms: "Thebes you honor as the highest of all cities, with your lightning-struck mother; and now, when the city with all its people is held fast in disease, come with purifying foot over the slopes of Parnassos, over the roaring straits of the sea" (1137–45).[13] In the sculpture and vase-painting of the archaic

---

11. For the vase see Carpenter, Dionysiac Imagery, plate 36B and his account, pp. 100–101.

12. See Simon Goldhill, "The Great Dionysia and Civic Ideology," in Winkler and Zeitlin, eds., Nothing to Do with Dionysus? 97–129, especially 98–106; see also my Dionysiac Poetics, 356–59. On Dionysos and the theater see P. E. Easterling, "A Show for Dionysos," in Easterling, ed., Cambridge Companion to Greek Tragedy (Cambridge 1997), chap. 2, especially 36–38, 44–53.

13. See also Sophocles, Antigone 147–54 and Oedipus Tyrannos 209–15.

and classical periods, including the metopes of the Parthenon, Dionysos joins in the gods' battle against the Giants, a symbolic conflict between chaos and order particularly popular after the Persian Wars.[14] As Iakkhos, the divine child associated with Demeter, goddess of grain and the fertility of the earth, he has a place in the goddess's important mystery cult at Eleusis at the southern border of Athens. By the late fifth century Dionysos also has mysteries of his own into which men and women can be initiated with the promise of a better life in the hereafter. He also has an important place in the elaborate mythology of the so-called Orphic mysteries, though their date is controversial. In an old mythical tradition Dionysos himself descends to Hades to bring back his mortal mother, Semelé. Recent archaeological discoveries have confirmed these chthonic and initiatory associations and given fresh significance to the puzzling statement of the pre-Socratic philosopher, Herakleitos (sixth-century B.C.E.), "Dionysos and Hades are the same."[15] Mystery religions and foreign cults, such as those of Bendis, Kybelé, or Sabazios, were becoming more popular in late fifth-century Athens; and scholars have suggested that Euripides is using the myth of Dionysos' arrival from the East as a way of exploring the malaise about these new divinities.[16]

Initiation into the mysteries of Dionysos has many resonances in the play. At his first miracle in the play, the shaking of the palace by earthquake (the so-called Palace Miracle, 671–701), his worshipers see a bright light; as Richard Seaford has shown at length, such visions of light are often a part of the mystic experience.[17] The Stranger's dressing of Pentheus as a maenad before leading him to his death on Mount Kitháiron probably evokes the robing of the initiand in such mystery rites. By changing his or her ordinary clothes for the special garments of the god's worship, the initiand takes off his old identity and is sym-

14. See Carpenter, *Dionysiac Imagery*, chapter 2, also Richard Seaford, ed., *Euripides, Cyclops* (Oxford, 1984), on lines 5–9.

15. Herakleitos, 22B15, in Hermann Diels and Walther Kranz, eds., *Die Fragmente der Vorsokratiker*, 5th ed., 2 vols. (Berlin, 1950–52). For a recent overview of Dionysos' connections with Hades and passage to the Underworld see Fritz Graf, "Dionysian and Orphic Eschatology: New Texts and Old Questions," and Susan Guettel Cole, "Voices from beyond the Grave: Dionysos and the Dead," both in Faraone and Carpenter, eds., *Masks of Dionysus*, 239–58 and 276–95 respectively. On initiation into the Dionysiac mysteries see Richard Seaford, "Dionysiac Drama and the Dionysiac Mysteries," *Classical Quarterly* 31 (1981), 252–75; idem, *Reciprocity and Ritual* (Oxford, 1994), 280–301; idem, ed., *Bacchae*, 39–44; Walter Burkert, *Ancient Mystery Cults* (Cambridge, Mass., 1987), 33–35, 95–97. See also my *Dionysiac Poetics*, 353–55, with the further bibliography there cited.

16. See H. S. Versnel, *Inconsistencies in Greek and Roman Religion I: Ter Unus.* (Leiden, 1990), 131ff.

17. For the initiatory elements discussed here see the references to Seaford's work above, note 15; also his comments on 606–609, 616–37, 912–76 (Greek line numbers) in his edition of the play.

bolically reborn into a new life as a devotee of these mysteries. Simultaneously, initiation brings a figurative death to one's past life. The
robing scene, then, along with its demonstration of the god's uncanny
power, "Most terrible and most gentle," also dramatizes Pentheus'
movement, as an initiand, into a realm of experience that he has denied and that is hidden from him.

These initiatory motifs, however, have their particular function in
the tragic action. Nothing in the play suggests a mystical rebirth or
renewal. In its tragic perspective initiation brings bloody death, not
rebirth. Like all the rituals enacted in the play, its positive meaning is
perverted.[18] The play disturbs us precisely because Dionysos' life-
enhancing and life-destroying powers stand so close to one another.
The bacchants, who voluntarily accept the god, experience the happiness that the opening ode promises. Having refused the blessings of
the god, the Thebans shown in the play experience his destructive side.
The vases show the nymphs in Dionysos' entourage both fondling and
destroying the same wild animals (usually fawns or wild felines);[19] thus
the play shows the Theban maenads abruptly turning from a paradisi-
acal mood of Golden Age harmony with nature (783–817) to an irresistible and uncontrollable frenzy of killing and plunder (843–77).

Inevitably, Dionysos' cult was far more restrained in practice than
the mythical representations might suggest.[20] The eating of raw flesh
described in the *Bakkhai's* first ode and hinted at after the *sparagmos*
of Pentheus (1339) is attested only once in the historical period, and
in a much milder and more banal form than in the play. In an inscrip-
tion from Miletos in the third century B.C.E. the worshipers are to
"throw in the piece of raw flesh," which may have consisted in token
bits of meat prepared and handed out in advance.

We should, then, be cautious about taking Euripides' portrait of the
god and his rites as a faithful indication of his cult in the ancient city-
state. Both the vases and the play are mythical representations, not
depictions of actual events. Nevertheless, such scenes do reveal an am-
bivalence about Dionysos in the Greek imaginary, that is, in the rep-
resentational forms that the ancient Greeks use to explore their con-
ceptual and emotional world. Dionysos is, as an anthropologist might
say, "good to think with" precisely because he calls into question the

---

18. On the ironic inversions of initiatory passage see my *Dionysiac Poetics*, chapter 6, and also
Helene Foley, *Ritual Irony* (Ithaca, N.Y., 1985) 208–18.

19. See Carpenter, *Dionysiac Imagery*, 114.

20. Jan N. Bremmer, "Greek Maenadism Reconsidered," *Zeitschrift für Papyrologie und Epigra-
phik* 55 (1984), 267–86; Albert Henrichs, "Greek Maenadism from Olympias to Messalina," *Har-
vard Studies in Classical Philology* 82 (1978), 121–60.

barriers between the animal and human realms and between the pulsing energies of nature and the order and discipline required for civilized life.

NOMOS AND *PHYSIS*: DIONYSOS AND "THE NATURAL"

The conflicts over Dionysos in the play implicate one of the major
philosophical and ethical debates of the late fifth century, the dichotomy between *nomos* and *physis*, terms of wide-ranging import for Euripides' contemporaries.[21] *Nomos* (law or custom) implies social practice and established institutions. *Physis* (usually translated nature) refers
to forces that are generally restrained by *nomos*: the instincts, the appetites, the demands and impulses of the body. *Physis* shows up culture
as an artificial imposition on something more basic or more essential
than human institutions. It includes those aspects of the natural world
that are beyond human control or not made by human design but to
which humankind may be subject. Contemporaries of Euripides use
arguments from *physis* to suggest the existence of dangerous, aggressive
traits in humankind that law has to keep in check, or to demonstrate
that law is an artificial constraint on underlying, amoral animal appetites we would all gladly indulge if we dared. The latter is the position
of the Unjust Argument of Aristophanes' *Clouds*, developed in a more
radical direction by Plato's Kallikles in the *Gorgias* and Thrasymakhos
in the *Republic*. Nature is here defined as a ruthless human will to
power that seeks domination wherever it can. But the *nomos-physis*
dichotomy can also take a more benign form, where the institutions of
society (*nomoi*) are seen as themselves rooted in nature (*physis*) or
where nature even offers relief from the restraints or the harshness of
certain social institutions.[22] Such theories attempt to bridge over the
gap between *nomos* and *physis*, and these too find resonances in the
Bakkhai.[23]

While Dionysiac worship has affinities with nature in releasing our
emotional energies and bringing us closer to the life force of plants
and animals, the play is far from extolling *physis* over *nomos*. Both the

---

21. For the *nomos-physis* dichotomy in the play and its relation to the Sophistic movement see
W. K. C. Guthrie, *A History of Greek Philosophy*, vol. 3 (Cambridge, 1969), 55–134; G. B. Kerferd,
The Sophistic Movement (Cambridge, 1981), 111–130. For a brief and lucid recent discussion see
Desmond Conacher, *Euripides and the Sophists* (London, 1998), 99–107.

22. These views resemble the respective positions of the so-called Anonymus Iamblichi (number
89, chapter 6, in Diels-Kranz, *Fragmente der Vorsokratiker*) and the controversial and fragmentary
On Truth attributed to Antiphon the Sophist (87 B44, in Diels-Kranz). For discussion see Guthrie
84–107 and Kerferd 115–16.

23. For some of the complexity of *nomos* and *physis* in the play see my *Dionysiac Poetics*, 20–22,
31, 344, and chapter 3 passim.

chorus and Teiresias, for instance, imply that Dionysos' worship brings law and nature together. At various points in the play, the chorus of Lydian bacchants, Kadmos, and Teiresias all urge the acceptance of the worship of Dionysos as part of the established laws or customs (*nomoi*) of the mass of the common people. As the chorus sings at the end of their second ode, "Whatever everyone, all / Simple, ordinary people, / Prefer and do, this I accept" (513–15). The chorus associates its god with ancient and widespread religious practices involving the joyful celebration of fertility, the vitality of nature, and the old Near Eastern earth- and mother-goddess, Kybelé. The prophet Teiresias has a more rationalistic approach; he appears, anachronistically, as an adherent of the fifth-century intellectual movement known as the Sophistic Enlightenment. For him Dionysos is virtually an allegory for the principle of liquid nurture, complementing Demeter, goddess of grain and agriculture (321–34; see also 236–40).

Near the end of its fourth ode, the third stasimon, the chorus makes its most explicit and most philosophical statement about this harmony between *nomos* and *physis* in Dionysiac cult (1022–27): "It costs so little / To believe that it does rule— / Whatever the divine may be, / Whatever over long ages of time / Is accepted as lawful, always, / And comes to be through nature."[24] On this view, Dionysiac religion allows the necessary release and expression of the animal energies that are part of nature but within the framework of the established social institutions, the *nomoi*.

Pentheus takes the opposite position: for him the *nomoi*, the institutions of society, are culture's necessary imposition on nature. He is suspicious and fearful of the dangers inherent in instincts and impulses that are not checked and channeled by social control. The followers of Dionysos might respond that these instincts are essential parts of human beings and so must be part of culture too. On this view the *nomoi* must make a place for this part of ourselves, otherwise culture itself is flawed and precarious. In other words, as lines 1022–27 (cited above) imply, *nomos* is itself grounded in *physis*. When the chorus repeatedly invokes sound good sense and wisdom (*sôphrosynê* and *sophia*), it refers to the balance between nature and culture, instincts and law, that exists when Dionysos has his proper place within the city. The wisdom that the chorus claims for its god (*sophia*) contrasts with the cleverness (*to sophon*) of its opponents who would exclude Dion-

---

24. The text and interpretation of these difficult but important lines follow E. R. Dodds, ed., Euripides, *Bacchae*, 2nd edition (Oxford, 1960), on 890–92, 893–94, 895–96 of Greek text

ysos and keep the city under a narrow, authoritarian definition of both law and culture (see 469, 1002–6).

The play, however, unsettles and destabilizes the two positions. Both sides claim the virtues of sound good sense and wisdom. But Pentheus, ostensibly defender of the laws of the city, is far from rational and is carried away by emotional violence and excess. The worshipers of Dionysos, initially at least, praise peace and calm; but the play's most spectacular manifestation of Dionysiac ecstasy is a wild and murderous vengeance and a mad lust for blood. Early in the play the young king, the old prophet of Thebes, and the Lydian representatives of Dionysos all claim the authority of *nomos*: all, in their own way, present themselves as defenders of culture. But by the end all three are in some way discredited, Pentheus by the repressiveness and self-blindness that accompanies his violence, Teiresias and Kadmos by their utilitarian rationalizations and interested motives (the glory of Thebes and the prestige of established religious authority), and the chorus by its increasing fanaticism and murderous vengefulness that its god, in the closing scenes, does nothing to mitigate.

RESISTANCE, EPIPHANY, AND ILLUSION

The *Bakkhai* tells the story of how Dionysos overcomes the resistance to his worship at Thebes, and it is a widespread story type in myths about the god. It is a tale of triumph but also a tale of pain. Aeschylus dramatized a similar myth in his trilogy about the Thracian king Lykourgos who rejects the worship of the god, is driven mad, and chops his son to bits with an ax thinking that he is attacking a vine sacred to the god.[25] Aeschylus wrote another trilogy on Dionysos' arrival at Thebes, which included a *Semelé* and a *Pentheus*. This myth, like all the myths that tragedy retells, could be rendered in a number of different ways. Euripides seems to have followed the outlines of Aeschylus' plot, but with more emphasis on the human psychology and perhaps also on the problematical side of divine justice.[26]

The *Bakkhai* dramatizes a recurrent mythical narrative in which a city refuses to accept Dionysos and he then turns its women against their own flesh and blood in bacchantic madness. After proving his divinity at Thebes through the filicidal madness of Agaüe, Dionysos

---

25. See Homer, *Iliad* 6.130–40 and Sophocles, *Antigone* 955–65.

26. For the Aeschylean plays about Dionysos see Dodds, ed., *Bacchae*, Introduction, xxviii–xxxiii; Seaford, ed., *Bacchae*, 26–28, with further bibliography. The hypothesis to Euripides' *Bakkhai* attributed to Aristophanes of Byzantium (third century B.C.E.) says, "The myth is found in the *Pentheus* of Aeschylus."

proceeds to Argos, where he similarly drives the women mad so that "on the mountains they devour the flesh of the children whom they held at the breast."[27] When the daughters of King Minyas at Orkhomenos ignore his festival and continue their sober women's work of weaving, the looms suddenly sprout vines and grapes and the room drips milk and honey. These women then rush forth to the mountain where one of them tears apart her child.[28] Similarly in the *Bakkhai* the Theban women leave the looms for the mountain and then abruptly change from sending forth wine, milk, and honey to shedding blood.[29] Such myths may reflect the power of the god to release women from the control of the patriarchal household;[30] but they also show how suddenly he can shift from fostering to destroying life. In the resistance myth of Lykourgos discussed above, for example, the king not only chops up his own son but also by his death restores the fertility of the land. In such myths of Dionysos, fertility and destructiveness are always dangerously close.

Theatricality is fundamental to Dionysiac ritual, with its masked dancers, choral performances, and processions of citizens who dress up as satyrs and march around with images of the phallus.[31] As god of the mask, Dionysos offers his worshipers the freedom to be other than themselves and so to engage in the playful license that characterizes his festivals.[32] The possibility of acting out another identity, of entering into a self that is not one's own, obviously underlies the dramatic performances that are an important part of those festivals. The mask can also be frightening: it is risky to step out of one identity into another. The remarkable scene in which the Stranger dresses the Theban king as a maenad—that is, as the ultimate Other as far as Pentheus is con-

27. Apollodorus, *Library of Mythology* 3.5.2. These Argive women are probably to be identified with the daughters of King Proetus, who in some versions are driven mad by Dionysos: see Apollodorus 2.2.2.

28. Aelian, *Varia Historia* 3.42; see also Ovid, *Metamorphoses* 4.389–415. The madness of Ino follows a similar pattern and, though sent by Hera, also has Dionysiac associations: see Apollodorus 3.4.3 and Ovid, *Metamorphoses* 4.520–30. See Burkert, *Greek Religion* 164; Seaford, *Reciprocity*, 291–92.

29. For the looms see *Bakkhai* 147–48; cf. 601, 1394–95, and for the change from nurturing liquids to bloodshed, and vice versa, see *Bakkhai* 166–77, 786–881.

30. On Dionysos and liberation of women from the household see Seaford, *Reciprocity*, 258–62, 301–11, 326–27; also his "Dionysos as Destroyer of the Household: Homer, Tragedy, and the Polis," in Carpenter and Faraone, eds., *Masks of Dionysus*, 115–46.

31. Seaford, *Reciprocity*, 266–75.

32. On Dionysos and the mask see Françoise Frontisi-Ducroux, *Le Dieux-masque: une figure de Dionysos à Athènes* (Paris, 1991); eadem, *Du masque au visage* (Paris, 1995), 105–16; Henrichs in Carpenter and Faraone, eds., *Masks of Dionysus*, 36–39; my *Dionysiac Poetics*, 372–73; Eric Csapo, "Riding the Phallus for Dionysos," *Phoenix* 51 (1997), 255–58, with references to earlier literature.

cerned—examines the danger and the pleasure of losing oneself in the power of illusion, including dramatic illusion.[33]

The late fifth century was much interested in the nature of artistic illusion, which, in any case, is associated with Dionysiac masking. This too finds dramatic enactment in the play. Thus as Pentheus here moves from the margins of the spectacle, as an onlooker, to its center as the hunted beast-victim, the scene also explores the process of surrendering to illusion. Although Pentheus stands initially in the place of the audience, as it were, eager to see the spectacle that the Stranger has offered to him, he soon becomes the central figure in the little drama of destruction that Dionysos has staged and for which he has dressed his "actor," Pentheus. The episode thus explores the crossing of the boundary between spectator and participant in a terrifying way.

Dionysos makes his presence felt among his worshipers in a burst of numinous energy that inspires awe, joy, and a sense of power. This sudden, mysterious appearance is a regular feature of his cult. Euripides draws on this cultic background in constructing his play as a sequence of epiphanies, each of which marks a new stage of the action.[34] Dionysos' first word, and the first word of the play in the Greek, hêkô, "I have come" or "I am here," suggests that the entire play can be viewed as his epiphany.[35] In the later epiphanies within the play, the god makes himself known miraculously in a blaze of light or, more ominously, in the form of an animal, particularly a bull. The signs of the god's presence gradually become stronger and more dangerous: from the Stranger's assertions of the god's presence in his face-to-face interrogation by Pentheus (537–607), to the "great light" accompanying the earthquake that shakes the palace and the bull-like phantom with which Pentheus wrestles in the dark enclosures of the palace (717–39).

When Pentheus later emerges from the palace robed as a maenad and is completely in the god's power, he sees the god in the form of a bull (1054–57). That scene ends with the chorus's prayer for a Dionysiac epiphany (1153–55): "Appear as a bull! As a snake / With many heads, for us to see you! / As a lion with a mane of fire!" The prayer

---

33. See my *Dionysiac Poetics*, chap. 7, with the Afterword, 369–78. To the references there cited add Easterling, ed., *Cambridge Companion to Greek Tragedy*, 165–73, 193–98; Mark Ringer, *Electra and the Empty Urn* (Chapel Hill, 1998); Gregory Dobrov, *Figures of Play: Greek Drama and Metafictional Poetics* (Oxford 1998).

34. The epiphanies and miraculous metamorphoses of the god are also prominent in the *Homeric Hymn to Dionysus* (Hymn 7 of the *Homeric Hymns*). See Henrichs in Carpenter and Faraone, eds., *Masks of Dionysus*, 16–22.

35. See Dodds, ed., *Bakkhai*, on line 1, p. 62; also Giorgio Ieranò, ed., *Euripide, Baccanti* (Milan, 1999), p. 98.

is answered in effect by the god's appearance in the Second Messenger's speech, which must have aroused the same frisson of horror and awe in the ancient audience as it still does today (1224–29): "And as the voice proclaimed these things, / A rising light of holy fire was set / Between the earth and heaven. The high air / Was still; the leaves of all the trees were still—/ You would not have heard one animal / Stir or cry out." The contrasting effect of these epiphanies corresponds to the contrasts in Dionysos throughout the play. To his worshipers they bring joy and relief; to outsiders, terror and danger.

Dionysos intensifies the power of his epiphanies by concealing his divine appearance beneath the guise of the Lydian Stranger. Even his disguising of Pentheus in his revenge plot is paradoxically a form of revelation as it brings to light a hitherto hidden side of the young king. Dressed and led as a maenad to the mountain, Pentheus loses his vaunted control over women and sexuality. Not only can he no longer control the boundaries between interior and exterior, city and mountain, self and other, but he can no longer control his own sexuality. The Lydian Stranger (Dionysos in disguise) gradually emerges as the young king's repressed alter ego, the side of himself that he would keep locked behind the fortified walls of his city or confined in the dark prison of the palace. Failing to do this, Pentheus suffers a fragmentation of self that, in the play's nightmare vision, is physically enacted in the *sparagmos*, the ritual rending of his body by the bacchants.

THE PLAY

Euripides begins this play, as he does several others, with a god who explains the background and describes the future course of events. This god, Dionysos, however, has taken on mortal form (5) and will be an actor in his own plot. His disguise also points to some of the unique qualities of Dionysos' cult: the importance of epiphany (the god's sudden revelation of himself to his worshipers), his closeness to his worshipers, and the intense closeness of his presence that he makes them feel—qualities that the following ode will soon exhibit.

Dionysos begins with the story of his birth. Semelé, daughter of Kadmos and sister of Agauë, became pregnant with Dionysos by Zeus. Hera, Zeus's jealous wife, tricks Semelé into asking her divine lover to appear before her in his full celestial splendor (Zeus being the god of the sky, lightning, and thunder); and she is killed by the lightning flash of this private epiphany. The results of Semelé's fatal request are still visible in the smoking ruin at Thebes that is now her tomb and her memorial, and Dionysos has made this burgeon with grapevines. Zeus saved the child by keeping him in the "male womb" of his thigh (the world's first incubator) until he was ready to be born (614–17). Dionysos, now a young god (as he generally is in late fifth-century representations),[36] has come to Thebes to vindicate his status as the son of Zeus, to punish the Theban royal family for refusing his worship, and to introduce his rites to Greece, beginning with his birthplace. He has driven mad Semelé's sisters, including Pentheus' mother Agauë, and along with them all the women of Thebes, and sent them outside the city to Mount Kitháiron (44–53). There, as the play begins, they are celebrating Dionysos' rites as the first bacchants of Greece.

As Dionysos concludes the prologue, the exotically dressed chorus of Asian bacchants enter the orchestra to the excited rhythms of flute (and perhaps drum) and proclaim its god in an exquisitely beautiful first ode (the parodos, 84–202). Calling to the bacchants to join the rites, the chorus display the distinctive features of this new god's worship: delight in song, ecstatic dancing, the excitement of pulsing animal life, and the forgetting of self in the surge of intense group emotion. The first real action of the play, however, shows a very different area of the god's power as the two elders of Thebes—the prophet Teiresias and the former King Kadmos—enter carrying the fawn skin and the thryrsos, emblems of Dionysos' worship, on their way to join his devotees on the mountain. The scene may have its comic aspect, but it also shows Dionysos' universal power. He transforms Thebes' most sober citizens to roles completely different from their accustomed ones. This is a modest and, so far, benign indication of the god's power to change radically those who acknowledge his power. But, as Pentheus now enters, the sight of the old men in Dionysiac dress infuriates him, and he ridicules both the worshipers and the god.

Pentheus' first lines on the stage (254–88) define the issues of his conflict with Dionysos: the city's control of women, sexuality, and the reinforcement of restraints and boundaries. He dwells on the seductive effects of the new cult on women and pays particular attention to the erotic attractions of the young Lydian Stranger (see 273–77). He will imprison the bacchants in the city, hunt down and put in chains those on the mountain, and have the Stranger's head, with its tossing hair, severed from his body. This very punishment will be Pentheus' own fate, in accordance with the play's basic structure of reversals between the young king and the young Stranger, aggressors and victims, active and passive figures, hunters and hunted.

36. Sixth-century representations of Dionysos show him as a mature adult with a full beard. By the last half of the fifth century he is shown as a graceful, beardless youth, as in the reclining figure (probably) on the east pediment of the Parthenon, around 440 B.C.E.

"Yet another wonder," Pentheus cries scornfully, when he sees the new converts. He at once puts the blame on Teiresias, threatens him with prison, and fulminates against the cult's corruption of women (289–306). The ridicule that Pentheus heaps on these male bacchants, however, will eventually be directed at him when he dons maenadic dress (1044–1105); and there the laughter will be mixed with the tragic emotions of pity and fear. In the carefully calibrated reversals, the god will laugh at him (1156; cf. 959, 973–74), and the "wonders" that he scorns (289) will soon attest the god's irresistible power (534, 773, 799, 822, 1203).

The Teiresias scene enacts one of the play's central problems: how to bring Dionysos and his cult into the city. It also inaugurates the pattern of verbal debate or contest (*agôn*) between a representative of the new god and his opponent. The old men offer a tame Dionysos, easily assimilable to the rational discourses of profit, utility, and allegorical interpretation. Pentheus' angry response quickly dispels the lecture-room atmosphere of Teiresias' speech and the grandfatherly mildness of Kadmos' admonitions. He escalates the violence, orders his attendants to destroy Teiresias' places of augury, reiterates his commands to imprison the bacchants and their leader, and condemns the Lydian Stranger to death by stoning—another punishment that will later turn back on himself (409–21; cf. 1240–42). Teiresias, in his turn, repeats his warnings about Pentheus' own madness; and the two elders exit as they entered, feebly stumbling off to make their way to Dionysos' rites on the mountain (428–32).

The choral ode that follows once more contrasts Pentheus' violence with the festive joy and beauty of a god associated with Holiness, love, the Muses, the vegetative fertility of nature, peace, plenty, and good sense. This Dionysos, far from disrupting the household, as Pentheus thinks, "will keep / The household safe and whole" (464 f.). The chorus utter a brief warning about Pentheus' "unbridled" mouth and lawless madness (457–59), but in general this is a serene and happy ode, and it forms the background to Pentheus' first face-to-face encounter with the Lydian Stranger, whose calm and self-control contrast sharply with the angry, excited young king (547–607). Pentheus' authority has already been challenged by his attendant's opening announcement that the imprisoned bacchants were miraculously freed (527–33). The ensuing *agôn* (contest) with the god/Stranger, now in the line-by-line exchange known as *stichomythia*, rather than in the set speeches of the previous scene, only increases Pentheus' bafflement and wrath. The ending of this contest exactly parallels the previous one: Pentheus once more issues orders of imprisonment, and his opponent exits with a warning about punishment from the god (595–607; cf. 406–35).

The next ode, the second stasimon (608–70), celebrates Dionysos' miraculous birth from the thigh of Olympian Zeus; but it also describes Pentheus as a savage monster, child of the earthborn Ekhion. This ode has a more threatening tone than the last as the chorus prays to the god to "end the insults of a murderous man" (651). Yet it returns to the beauty of Dionysiac song in lush poetry that associates Dionysos with an Orphic closeness to nature, fertilizing water, and vegetative life (652–70).

This radiant evocation of Dionysos leading his maenads over the mountains and rivers of northern Greece is suddenly interrupted by the god's cry, "Io! / Io Bakkhai! Io Bakkhai! Hear me, hear my voice!" (671–72), which resumes the excited mood of the chorus's opening song ("Onward, Bakkhai! Onward, Bakkhai!" 157–58). Dionysos now displays his power in his first epiphany; and the mysterious collapse of the palace and accompanying flashes of light and fire in this Palace Miracle introduce the next *agôn* between god and king (671–701). Whether or not the palace actually collapses and how such an event might have been staged remain disputed: the palace seems intact in the scene between Kadmos and Agauë at the end of the play. In any case, Dionysos has begun to reveal himself for the power that he is; and that power includes his irresistible spell, whether of ecstasy, illusion, or madness.

Now the tables are turned, and Pentheus is stymied at every move. Dionysos (continuing in the guise of the Lydian Stranger) takes control of the narrative and the stage action as he encourages his recently imprisoned bacchants (the chorus) and describes the events inside (710–40). The brief face-to-face encounter that follows again focuses on the issue of boundaries and enclosure as Pentheus shouts, "I order the circle of walls and towers completely closed!" (757). But, as the previous scene has shown, the god infiltrates the defenses of the city and the palace as mysteriously as he begins to infiltrate the defenses of Pentheus' mind.

The face-to-face conflict is interrupted by a sudden shift to the realm outside those city boundaries, the wilds of Mount Kitháiron where the women of Thebes are now raging as maenads. The god has thus destroyed Pentheus' control over the boundaries of his realm in two complementary directions: He has liberated his own Lydian bacchants from the palace within the city, and he has sent the Theban women outside the walls to be maenads on the mountain. The abrupt reversal within the maenads' behavior there, from Golden Age bliss to a frenzy of bloodshed (783–881), anticipates the bloody reversal soon to afflict Pentheus and Agauë. The Messenger's account at first only hardens Pentheus in his resistance to the god. The long scene between Pentheus and the Stranger that follows then repeats the structure of the previous contests, an *agôn* between the god's representative and his antagonist that soon turns into a tense, line-by-line verbal duel (893–963).

In this succession of conflictual scenes, Dionysos increasingly displays his power, and Pentheus increasingly displays his vulnerabilities. We recall that Pentheus is a youth (321, 1110), almost beardless (1340–42), is still unmarried, and cannot have been king for very long. His mildness (relatively speaking) toward Kadmos and Kadmos' corresponding gentleness toward him in his first stage appearance may even evoke a certain sympathy and lay a basis for greater sympathy later.[37] Pentheus makes the wild threats characteristic of the stage tyrant, but for all his bluster he remains an ineffectual youth. He fails in all of the threats that he makes in the course of the play. When he calls out Thebes' armed forces in response to the news of the women on the mountain (896–902), the troops seem not to arrive. When he acknowledges his failure to keep the Stranger in prison, his renewed threat of punishment is almost laughable (909–10): "Will you stop lecturing me and—since you've escaped your bonds—/ Hold onto your freedom? Or I'll punish you again!"

Dionysos checks Pentheus' furious (but futile) energy by unexpectedly asking, "Do you want to see [the maenads] sitting together on the mountain?" (928), and Pentheus is suddenly under his spell. In this quiet and terrible moment the god asserts his power over his antagonist through the mysterious bond that he has always known was there between them. Pentheus surrenders to something in himself as well as in Dionysos. Dionysos hints at an offer to bring the women and "save" Pentheus; but, just when Pentheus seems to break free of the Stranger's allure by ordering his attendants to bring his weapons instead, the Stranger utters the single syllable "Aaah!" outside of the regular meter, and then makes the offer that Pentheus cannot resist. With a single word the god exposes and releases all the longings that Pentheus has fought against in himself. In fact, his loss of self-control plays directly into his opponent's hands, for it reveals that emotional vulnerability by which Dionysos will destroy him.

Pentheus leaves the stage muddled and undecided (962–63): "I think that I'll go in. For I must either / Proceed against them armed, or suffer

---

37. Although Pentheus sees Kadmos' dress as laughable and warns him not to rub off his madness on him (291–92, 406–8), he lays the blame chiefly on Teiresias (296–306), against whom he rages furiously—in the manner of Creon in the *Antigone* and Oedipus in the *Oedipus Tyrannos*—while he has gentler words for Kadmos (293–96; cf. 408), and Kadmos addresses him in a similar way (389–405).

your advice."[38] His conversion from resistance to surrender is bracketed by his two statements about taking up arms (926, 962–63). The hesitation itself marks a radical change from the determined and impetuous energy of his previous responses to the god. The discrepancy between his bluster and his inaction shows a king no longer fully in control either of his city or himself and foreshadows his ignominious defeat. By even entertaining the Stranger's proposition, Pentheus has already mentally exchanged the male warrior's weapons for the female devotee's dress and cap.

This passage is a masterpiece of characterization in its depiction of the Stranger's role as Pentheus' repressed alter ego; it is also central for the reversals of gender roles that underlie the action. Throughout the play Pentheus has insisted on rigidly defined categories of space, age, and gender. In this scene he considers it the greatest possible shame if "what we're made to suffer/ We should suffer at the hands of women" (901–2). Dionysos, who has already demonstrated his epithet Lysios, "the one who releases," to the imprisoned bacchants, also "releases" men and women from the constraints of their usual roles and views of themselves. The aged Kadmos and Teiresias, we recall, feel restored to youth in their zeal to worship the god. Now the Stranger changes Pentheus from warrior to maenad as he leads him from the city gates and walls to the mountain forests and streams.

On the mountain the women are not only free of male supervision but, as hunters and warriors, take over the attributes of male power. In the more benign side of that freedom, they turn from domestic work and confinement in the house (weaving at the loom and nursing their infants) to suckling wild animals (805–9). More radically still, the nurturing function of the domesticated female body turns outward miraculously to make streams of water, wine, milk, and honey spurt or flow from the earth (811–17). Both scenes enact a kind of Dionysiac maternity, redirecting maternal energy from culture to nature in a generosity that breaks down the boundaries between human and animal. The women leave their traditional and socially useful roles in the patriarchal household for a supernatural communion with nature in an all-female society in the wild. Yet to come is the nightmarish perversion of female roles when the mother kills her son and takes him back into her own body in the Dionysiac feast (1338–39).

For Pentheus the victory of Dionysos means not merely the disso-

---

38. Pentheus' confusion in 963 is conveyed in part by the ambiguity of the word translated as suffer *peisomai*, which means both I shall obey (from *peithô*) and I shall suffer (from *paschô*): see my *Dionysiac Poetics*, 251–53.

lution of all the boundaries and divisions that he has so intensely defended. It also involves a regression from the role of adult king and warrior to confused adolescent and finally to infantile helplessness before a raging, all-powerful mother. When he capitulates to Dionysos' temptation, he not only yields to a voyeuristic sexuality (of which his mother is, in part, the object) but also moves backward from the status of hoplite warrior—that is, the armor-wearing adult citizen-soldier—to the status of the ephebe. The ephebe is the youth between the ages of eighteen and twenty who carries light weapons and has the particular task of patrolling the mountainous frontier country as a scout and a "spy." Hence, when Pentheus is unable to take up those "arms" in 926 and 962–63 and instead agrees to become a spy using guile and concealment on the mountain (955, 1048–50, 1088–89), he fails at a major point of male generational passage and is fixated at the ephebic stage. Simultaneously, he becomes the hunted instead of the hunter, a woman instead of a man, the sacrificial victim instead of the sacrificer, a beast instead of a human being, and the despised scapegoat instead of the powerful king.[39] Symmetrical with Pentheus' collapse of identity is Dionysos' victorious assertion of his. In his call to the women at the end of the scene, the Stranger, though addressing Dionysos, comes close to breaking out of his disguise and resuming his divine identity, as he foretells Pentheus' humiliation and death at his mother's hands (964–80).

The ode that follows Pentheus' surrender and incipient defeat celebrates the beauty of Dionysiac freedom (981–1001). The maenads can now dance like a fawn leaping in the green woods as it joyfully outruns the hunter and his hounds (981–1043). But, as the ode goes on, it exemplifies a combination of beauty and vengeance analogous to Dionysos' own combination of gentleness and fearfulness (979–80). "But those whose lives are happy/ Day by day—those/ I call the blessèd," the chorus conclude (1041–43), as the Stranger ushers Pentheus out of the palace in the maenadic dress that is the sign of just how unfortunate his life will prove to be on this day.

As Pentheus shifts from fulminating ruler to obedient maenad and from the god's antagonist (*theomakhos*) to his sacrificial victim, the balance between what is "most gentle" and "most terrible" in the god also begins to shift (979–80). The odes of the first half of the play primarily depict Dionysos' liberating exuberance, whereas those of the

---

39. There are numerous hints at Pentheus' change from king to sacrificial victim: 910–11, 976–77; cf. 954, 1069.

concluding section are increasingly preoccupied with vengeance.[40] In the fifth and last full ode that the chorus sing, the fourth stasimon (1113–59), murderous thoughts predominate. The Lydian bacchants demonize the now helpless young king as a dangerous monster whose throat they would slit in self-righteous fury (1125–32). In the second stasimon this hatred was mitigated by the closing epode, with its lyrical evocations of the beauty of nature and Orphic song (contrast 630–38 and 652–70). Now there is no alleviating gentleness. Whereas the earlier epiphany brought a comforting light and freedom to oppressed worshipers (cf. 706–7), this new epiphany is destructive (1220–60).

The escalation of the vengeance from the Palace Miracle to the tearing apart of Pentheus, to be sure, is the inevitable consequence of the king's failure to heed the earlier and milder manifestations of Dionysos' power. Yet the justice of the punishment does not lessen its horror. The fourth stasimon, the prelude to the god's bloody vengeance, seems to belong to a world totally different from the lyrical beatitudes of the opening ode; yet these are the same bacchants. The god whose epiphany they invoke in the form of bull, snake, or lion is to show a "laughing face" as he hobbles his foe beneath the murderous herd of his maenads (1153–59). The bloody hunting and eating of raw flesh that belonged to the joyful ecstasy of the chorus's entering ode (169–71) now show their darker colors.

The maenads in the Second Messenger's speech, like those of the First Messenger's speech, begin with "pleasant tasks" as they entwine their thyrsoi with ivy and sing bacchantic songs to one another (1190–93). Yet their benign side is now much more limited. The liquid abundance of the first speech—the wine, honey, and milk spouting from the earth—has no place here; and the water of this setting is part of a harsher, more dangerous landscape, dominated by enclosing ravines and fir trees (1189–91, 1239–46). So too the maenads' change to murderous fury is much more abrupt as the god excites them to vengeance. His power now totally dwarfs his mortal opponents and worshipers. Whereas he had no direct intervention in the first scene on Kitháiron, now he makes his will known in an awesome, mystical moment that binds heavens to earth in a flash of light and brings silence to the whole forest (1224–29). The *sparagmos* (ritual tearing apart) that follows is as bloody as before, but now the victim is a designated human being, not a cow or bull, and the agents are not the collective band but the

---

40. See my *Dionysiac Poetics*, 243–44, 385; also Hans Oranje, *Euripides' Bacchae: The Play and Its Audience*, Mnemosyne Supplement 78 (Leiden, 1984), 101–13, 168–70.

victim's mother and aunts. Euripides spares us none of the horror. Pentheus begs in vain for mercy as he stares up into Agaue's rolling eyes and foaming mouth; the maenads play ball with the torn flesh; and Agaue finally carries the head impaled on the top of her thyrsos and parades it over the mountain as a triumphant huntress (1263–1301).

The Messenger ends with a few lines of cautious generalization about moderation, good sense, and piety toward the gods (1302–7). In the studied symmetries of this play, these lines correspond to the First Messenger's closing generalizations about the blessings of Dionysos (882–88). That First Messenger directly addressed Pentheus and praised Dionysos as the giver of wine, without which there is no sex "nor anything of pleasure for us mortals" (885–89). The Second Messenger ends with the "wisdom" of "piety and good sense" rather than with what is "pleasurable" (1304–7). With Pentheus' death, the mood is defensive rather than hedonistic. The chorus' behavior is also different. In responding to the First Messenger, it was far more hesitant and merely praised Dionysos as inferior to none of the gods (890–92). Now it is openly defiant, bursting out in lyrical exultation to celebrate the death of its opponent with shouting and dancing (1308–10). This outcry marks the maenads' total victory, but the emotional intensity is also carefully framed by a formal symmetry. The Messenger began his speech with a reference to the serpent-born ancestry of the Theban royal line, and the chorus takes that up at the end (cf. 1161–63 and 1310). The Messenger had been outraged when the chorus rejoiced at the sufferings of his master (1172–77); the chorus's lyrics now give free rein to that exultation; and there is no voice of protest to hold them back.

This scene brings home how different is this chorus's behavior from the usual role of the chorus in Greek tragedy. Far from identifying with the polis or with a communal voice of familiar moral generalizations, this chorus shockingly opposes the polis and so leaves the play without a voice of collective concern or normative civic morality.[41] At the end of the third stasimon, for example, we are uncertain how to reconcile the chorus's commonplaces about divine punishment and the vicissitudes of mortal life with its role as Lydian devotees of an ecstasy-inducing god. The ambiguity of its role in this respect corresponds to the ambiguities surrounding Dionysos' place in the polis that the play explores.

The Messenger, whether out of fear or pity, is eager to be off before

41. On this aspect of the chorus see my essay, "Chorus and Community in Euripides' *Bacchae*," in Lowell Edmunds and Robert W. Wallace, eds., *Poet, Public, and Performance in Ancient Greece* (Baltimore, 1997), 65–86.

Agauë returns (1302–3), and we now see her on the stage for the first time. Back from the mountain, she displays the grisly hunting trophy, her son's head, with which she intends to adorn the palace. The scene is the visual climax of Dionysos' inversions of Pentheus' world. Not only does Agauë take on the usual male roles of victorious warrior and triumphant hunter, but the victory song that she shares with the chorus is also a cruel parody of funerary lament, which often takes just this form of a lyrical exchange between a single woman and a choral group.[42] This unknowingly bereaved mother here utters cries of joy rather than of mourning. There are hints too of sacrificial inversion as Agauë invites the chorus to share this feast (1338–39); and we recall that the Messenger described her as priestess (*hierea*) as she "began the slaughter" of Pentheus (1262–63).

Like a proud, victorious warrior, Agauë takes her position before the palace, addresses the citizens of Thebes, and displays her victory trophy, the head that she would affix to the palace walls that Pentheus had so frenetically defended (1358–70). When Kadmos enters with the mutilated body, Agauë, still under the god's spell, holds Pentheus' head in her arm and boasts of her triumph in the traditional terms of masculine prowess. In a cruel irony, she wishes that her absent son could take after his mother in hunting (1411–14). Kadmos gradually leads her back to sanity in a line-by-line exchange (*stichomythia*) that has been compared to the process of bringing someone out of a psychotic episode.[43] It may be that in Macedon Euripides witnessed such techniques for bringing maenads back to sanity.

At this point the text has suffered some disruption (for the second half of the play there is only one surviving manuscript); the following scene, known as the *Compositio Membrorum*, or putting together of the limbs, is fragmentary. We can, however, reconstruct a good deal of it from various ancient sources and from the (probably) late Byzantine play, *The Passion of Christ* (*Christus Patiens*), which drew heavily on the *Bakkhai* (see Appendix, pp. 138–141). Agauë must have fit the head to the rest of the corpse and joined Kadmos in piecing the body together and lamenting over it. The scene is unexampled in Greek tragedy, and there is considerable controversy about how it was staged. Agauë's lament, which is almost entirely lost, must have been intensely emotional. Kadmos is more formal as he praises his grandson as the ruler of Thebes who always protected the old man (1491–1505); but the

---

42. Lines 1316–19, at the end of the strophe, prepare for this anomalous combination of the tears of the funeral dirge and the joyful shout of the victory celebration. See above, n. 10, p. 9.
43. See George Devereux, "The Psychotherapy Scene in Euripides' *Bacchae*," *Journal of Hellenic Studies* 90 (1970), 35–48.

funeral eulogy contrasts ironically with the death of a youth who has only threatened battle against the women of his household and is killed by female maenad-hunters, not male warriors.

At the end of the lament Dionysos appears as *deus ex machina*, presumably now in his Olympian form and no longer in disguise, and speaks from the roof of the stage building, or *theologeion*, which is often used for such scenes. The first part of his speech is lost, but the extant portion reveals a tone of harshness and self-vindication rather than compassion or understanding. He commands the exile of both Agauë and Kadmos. Agauë, polluted with the blood of her child, cannot remain in the city; Kadmos, along with his wife Harmonia will become serpents, lead an Illyrian tribe against Greek cities, and attack Apollo's shrine at Delphi. Here, as often in his endings, Euripides incorporates other parts of the mythical tradition. For Kadmos there is an additional irony. This founder of a Greek city who came originally from the barbarian (non-Greek) land of the Phoenicians and killed the serpent that guarded the spring of Dirké at Thebes will be turned into a serpent to lead barbarian hordes against Greek cities. For a Greek of this period exile is a terrible fate, depriving him or her of political power, civil rights, and family associations and protection. There is a small glimmer of light as Dionysos foretells Kadmos' eventual translation to the land of the blest, but this does not shine very brightly in the gloom of pollution, exile, and separation.

The gods of Greek tragedy do not pardon; and their retributive justice is not necessarily commensurate with the offense. Pentheus, like Lykourgos in the earlier resistance myth, provokes the god's wrath by the vehemence of his opposition and meets his inevitable end. Even the acceptant Kadmos is punished: although he accepted the god, he did not do so in the right spirit. Similarly, the suffering of Agauë and her sisters, like that of the daughters of Minyas at Orkhomenos, seems out of proportion to their offense, their initial doubts about the god in the prologue (33–43). Kadmos feebly protests that gods should be above mortal anger, but Dionysos attempts no moral justification and merely claims an ancient decree from Zeus and commands quick obedience to the necessity of "what you must do" (1565–68). In the old myths, Dionysos' revenge by murder within the family is cruel and brutal, and perhaps the audience would have regarded it as merely the traditional punishment. Yet Euripides introduces a criticism of anthropomorphic divinity that is not answered. As elsewhere, he leaves us with the incomprehensibility of the gods' justice and the gap between human and divine perspectives.

The play closes with a pathetic farewell between the aged grandfather and the grieving mother of Pentheus. The two mortal survivors are crushed by the catastrophe and by their impending exile. Like Hippolytos and Theseus at the end of the *Hippolytos*, they cling to one another for solace before they are forced to part forever. The play has shown us the beauty of those rites, but the closing scene also forces us to think about their other side.

The last words are reserved for Agauë (leaving aside the banal choral tag, which may be a later addition). Her only wish is to rejoin her sisters, sharers in her exile, and to have no further contact with bacchantic ritual. The movement is centrifugal and the mood funereal, especially if the request of her penultimate line, to be led "where no reminding thyrsos has been dedicated," evokes the tomb (1607).[44] The play ends with women, female experience, and the bacchants of the title; but Agauë's final line, "Let such things be for other Bakkhai" (1608), gives an ambiguous welcome to the future cult.

We cannot know how this closing scene was staged, but Pentheus' torn body, whether carried off at the end or left behind as Kadmos and Agauë exit, remains a powerful, inescapable image. It evokes, among other things, the horror of a whole family's extirpation as we see the doom of three generations of the royal line before us.[45]

DIONYSIAC ANAGNORISIS

The ending of the play exemplifies something in the experience of Dionysos that we may call a Dionysiac anagnorisis (recognition): wild abandon and exultation followed by a sad reawakening to a painful reality. In everyday terms, this is the experience of recovering from the wine-induced happiness of the god's gift, that is, a hangover. But in the action of the play this recognition is enacted first in a relatively gentle way in the Theban maenads' return from the mountain (877–81); then more grimly for Pentheus (see below) and when Agauë comes out of the Dionysiac ecstasy and realizes what she has done; and finally when Kadmos' bacchantic joy in the freedom from old age, which was

---

44. Seaford ed., *Bacchae*, on line 1386, citing 1157. Seaford on line 1387 (1608 here), however, would find in the reference to "other Bacchants" a dramatization of "the aetiological myth of D[ionysos'] cult at Thebes." But the mood is certainly not that of triumphant celebration of the founding of a new cult but rather the speaker's sense of loss and despair. For Esposito, for example, on 1387 (p. 91), "Agave's rejection of Dionysos and his devotees could not be more emphatic and in this final rejection she carries on the spirit of her son."

45. We are not told explicitly that the royal line is wiped out, but the play suggests as much, especially as it refers several times to the death of Pentheus' cousin, Aktaion, son of Agauë's sister, Ino. The image of the three destroyed generations at the end is the reverse of that of *Odyssey* 24.514–15, where old Laertes rejoices at the three generations of his restored household standing together in victorious battle against their enemies.

the first stage action of the play (203–53), gives way to the acknowledgment of his impotence as an "old man" (1502, 1572, 1584–87).

This Dionysiac anagnorisis differs in tone from the kind of anagnorisis that Oedipus, for example, experiences at the end of Sophocles' *Oedipus Tyrannos*. Oedipus, having blinded himself to the visible world, gains a deeper insight into the invisible powers surrounding his life and, more broadly, into the tragic nature of the human condition. In his journey from illusion to reality he gains a clearer understanding of the deceptive surface of appearances amid which he has lived and ultimately a new inner strength (see *Oedipus Tyrannos* 1414–15, 1455–58). When Agauë and Kadmos awaken from illusion they can discern only their utter misery and their helplessness before the divine power that has destroyed them. Pentheus emerges from the god's spell only long enough to recognize his imminent death at the hands of his murderous mother and aunts. He never discovers who the Stranger really is, nor does he gain any insight into the causes of his suffering. "And he will know that Dionysos, son/ of Zeus, was born a god in full," the god himself (in disguise) predicted, as he leads Pentheus to his death (978–80). But at the end of the next scene Pentheus leaves the stage in a quasi-hypnotic trance, and the narrative of his death is silent about his learning anything about the god. Agauë and Kadmos perceive more; but the psychological rather than the intellectual aspect of their recognitions is dominant; and the shock and horror overshadow the glimmers of a deeper moral understanding.

"Be sensible and revere all that belongs to the gods," the Second Messenger advises as he reports the results of the Theban maenads' liberation on the mountain (1307); but this moralizing solution is hardly adequate to the tragic experience that the play enacts. Throw off your chains and be free, Dionysos tells his worshipers; but the play then dramatizes the process of awakening to the horrors that this freedom has perpetrated. In their fresh enthusiasm for celebrating Dionysos early in the play Kadmos and Teiresias joyfully forget their age and feel young again (223–26). In bringing Agauë out of her madness, however, Kadmos again takes on the full weight of his years and the sad wisdom that goes with his age. Still under the god's spell, she reproaches her father for the killjoy crabbedness of his years (1410–11): "Old age in humankind is so ill-tempered,/ And has such scowling eyes!" But he rightly counters her bacchantic madness with a knowledge that consists in groans and a truth that consists in misery (1448): "Unhappy truth, how wrong the moment when you come to us!"

The myth of Oedipus, as Sigmund Freud suggested in a celebrated discussion, is at some level about the necessary restraints that Culture imposes on the residues of our animality.[46] Its divinity, Apollo, is a god who enforces limits and insists on the boundaries between mortality and divinity, between bestiality and humanity. The myths surrounding Dionysos, however, explore the liberation of our animality and the freedom from the repressive constraints of Culture. If the Oedipus myth shows happiness to be a tragic illusion, Dionysos celebrates the place of wine, joy, and festivity in human life; and, as the *Bakkhai* several times remarks, Dionysos' gifts accompany those of Aphrodite (493–96, 887–89). If the Oedipus myth demonstrates the disastrous consequences of breaking down differentiation, the myths around Dionysos exult in a joyous closeness of humans to the world of nature and animals. Dionysos, then, would seem to have a natural affinity to comedy; and this is true to the extent that numerous comedies and satyr plays use Dionysos, or Dionysiac figures, as their major characters. Yet, as the Dionysos trilogies of Aeschylus also indicate, the relation of Dionysos to Culture is deeply a tragic theme.

Euripides raises, but does not fully answer, the question of how to enjoy the Dionysiac intoxication without the wildness followed by horrified recognition. One answer, as I have suggested elsewhere, may lie in the god's other gift to Athens, not the maenadic ritual (unattested for Attica) but the gentler ecstasy of the dramatic performances at the festivals in honor of Dionysos, for these bring the god Dionysos safely into the polis and combine the pleasures of freedom with "calm" or "serenity" (*hêsychia*), abandon and ecstasy with emotional balance or sound mind (*sôphrosynê*). Here the recognition of truth brings cathartic integration rather than horror, madness, and pollution.[47]

Dionysos' explosive revelations of his identity change the world and worldview of the mortals he encounters. The reversals of strong and weak, persecutor and persecuted, so essential to the structure of the play, also raise the fundamental problem of where our sympathies lie. The first half of the play makes it easy for us to sympathize with the Stranger and his entourage against his overexcited persecutor, who behaves as the typical stage tyrant (compare Creon in the *Antigone*). But, as the god's revenge spreads from the now helpless Pentheus to Agauë and Kadmos, our view of Dionysos becomes more complicated. The audience knows that the god will triumph and that his cult, with its blessings and its dangers, will enter Thebes and thence all of Greece. Yet the play remains divided between the beauty of these rites, con-

---

46. See, for example, S. Freud, "Preface to Theodor Reik, *Ritual: Psycho-Analytical Studies*" (1919), in James Strachey, ed., *The Standard Edition of the Complete Psychological Works of Sigmund Freud*, vol. 17 (London, 1955), 261.

47. See my *Dionysiac Poetics*, 339–47.

veyed in the lyrics of the first four odes, and the ruthlessness of the god's vengeance as it unfolds at the end. We never feel that Pentheus is right. Presumably a less vehemently hostile response would have averted the catastrophe. Yet, like many Greek tragedies, the *Bakkhai* makes us feel both the inexorability of divine justice and pity for the human victims.

Euripides calls Dionysos that complex of impulses and energies in ourselves that can suddenly swing from joyful exultation to wild, savage murderousness. Total surrender to the ecstasy of group emotion in religious observance is beautiful and exalting; but, as both Euripides' era and our own know all too well, the breakdown of inhibitions in mass emotion can also lead "normal" men and women to atrocities of almost unimaginable horror. Proving himself a god — that is, an eternal, elemental power and an existential force — Dionysos also demands that we recognize and come to terms with his place in our world.

ACKNOWLEDGMENTS

I am chiefly responsible for the Introduction, Notes, Appendix, and most of the Glossary, but Reginald Gibbons and I have shared our views on nearly every aspect of the play, and I have profited greatly from his sensitivity to language, tone, and dramatic situation. I thank him for a collaboration that has also held the warmth of friendship. Peter Burian, series editor, and Oxford University Press editor Susan Chang helped with constructive criticism, encouragement, and patience. Like all those who have worked closely with the *Bakkhai*, I am painfully aware of how controversial many of its basic features remain. I owe many debts, which I could not fully acknowledge in this volume, to all of the commentators who have struggled with these problems and especially with the multiple and often contradictory features of Dionysos, notably E. R. Dodds, Albert Henrichs, and Richard Seaford. Specialists will see at once how indebted I am to their scholarship. Giorgio Ieranò kindly sent me a copy of his newly published Italian translation (with introduction and notes) at a timely moment.

Early drafts of my work on the play were done during my tenure as the Marta Sutton Weeks Senior Fellow at the Stanford Humanities Center of Stanford University in 1997–98, an honor for which I am deeply grateful. The work has also been sustained by the loving support of my wife, Nancy Jones, and enriched by the imaginative transformations of Greek myth by my daughter Cora, who has made Semelé a household word in ways that Euripides would never have foreseen.

Cambridge, Mass.   CHARLES SEGAL
August 2000

ON THE TRANSLATION

THE TEXT
I have based this translation on the editions of the Greek text by E. R. Dodds (1960) and Richard Seaford (1996), on reference to translations by classicists, including those by Seaford himself, Stephen Esposito, William Arrowsmith, and others, on the extensive scholarship in Dodds's notes to his edition, and on Charles Segal's *Dionysiac Poetics and Euripides' Bacchae* (1997) and his specific suggestions for this new version of the play.

Charles Segal has supplied me with his reconstruction of the gaps in the surviving Greek text, which I have versified. (For further details on the lacunae, see his Appendix, pp. 134–41.) Brackets in the translation mark major conjectural or reconstructed passages, but many smaller such passages are presented without brackets, to avoid cluttering the English-language text.

TRANSLATING THE LANGUAGE OF THE PLAY
In this translation I have tried to leave the reader with what will seem convincing and authoritative to the mind and the ear without need of additional comment. So the following remarks are for the reader with an interest in the problems of translation and curiosity about the poetic form of the Greek text.

From John Herington's account of the origins of Greek tragedy (*Poetry into Drama: Early Tragedy and the Greek Poetic Tradition*, University of California Press, 1985), I understand the whole play as a very long poem in several parts that differ from each other in terms of diction, poetic line, and structure. Although I cannot represent in the translation the different Greek meters and poetic forms that Euripides used, I have tried to compose the different parts (dialogue, narrative, odes) in distinguishable ways. (More about meter, later.) I have tried to find language that represents the Greek as closely as I can do so in order to give some flavor of the compression and metaphoric intensity of the original, while at the same time producing an English that is idiomatic, however distant it may be, especially in the odes, from speech. In fact, the Greek of the tragedies in ancient Athens was a language used only on stage, in performance, not in daily life, nor was it based on the dialect of Greek that Athenians spoke. So I should probably have sought even more strangeness in the English translations in order not to misrepresent the linguistic color of the original.

I hope that all the lines of the translation are both sayable and play-able; yet I also sought to get a certain small resistance into them, which is the residue of their overdetermined meaningfulness and linguistic peculiarity, that is mostly absent from real speech in real life. To trans-late the play in such a way as to make it *most* sayable, for the sake of idiomatic and even colloquial speech (which is *not* what the Greek stage emphasized, but *is* how we play most of our dramas in our con-temporary world), would be to lose some of the intricate pattern of repeated words and formulaic modifiers, figures of speech, and mean-ingful periphrasis. To translate the play in such a way as to preserve as much as possible of the word repetition, wordplay, formulas, and fig-urative language would be to lose, for the sake of the rich linguistic texture and literariness of the drama, some of its playability. In between lie ways of compromise that may produce, if only linguistic luck can equal the translator's labor, some measure of both dimensions of this ancient drama as a work in our own, present-day language. There's nothing new about this problem of translating a Greek drama except that in translating Euripides' *Bakkhai* I myself happened to be the translator who was caught inside it, and my translation is my attempt to solve it.

As is often the case in the most remarkably integrated and richly signifying literary works, it seems that nearly every single word in *Bak-khai* not only plays its small role in this or that unfolding sentence, but also adds meaning to the work as a whole—an effect that makes study of this work a process of gradually becoming aware of patterns of interrelated words, images, dramatic situations, kinship relations, and other elements as well as of ceaselessly moving one's attention back and forth between each detail and the whole. (Fittingly, this movement of our literary attention was long ago christened by philological criti-cism with a word derived from ancient Greek, *hermeneutic*—from the name of Hermes, the minor immortal who served as messenger of the Greek gods, circulating among them and between them and mortals.)

Inevitably, in a work so richly meaningful, word by word, and written with such compressed syntax and with such a multitude of figures of speech, every decision in translation has to be interpretive. And this particular drama has given rise to uncertain, contradictory, and disputed interpretations. For one reason or another, many of the key Greek words in the play either remain ambiguous or had a meaning for the ancient Greeks that we cannot confidently establish for ourselves, living as we do in a different culture that has lost close contact with nearly every aspect of the material culture and ways of thinking and believing of the Greeks. We have the privilege of being able to see the remains of ancient Greek culture, but we cannot return entirely to the Greek mind. And we are also in the odd position of seeing an ancient word not only as itself but also in the light of all that it turned into, in later centuries, as it evolved and gathered around itself meanings and associations that are entirely extraneous to its Greek meanings and associations. So in hearing words like *wisdom, happiness, initiation, sound mind, nature,* and others, how can we get very free of *our* customary meanings and find a Greek meaning?

Furthermore, Euripides turns many words to an ironic meaning as he stages the contest of will between Dionysos and Pentheus, the illusions of Pentheus and Agauë, and the rationales of Teiresias and Kadmos, so he too is *already* putting into question the meanings that were evident to the Greeks. There are many puns and double meanings, words put into etymological play, poetic devices. Also, because the syntax of Euripides' Greek is extraordinarily compressed, a translation into English requires more words and lines than did the original.

Euripides also puts the play's figures into situations in which illusion and reality, the mind of the god, the ancient Greek experience of divinity, and the meaning of the action are not only subject to disagreement among us, today—because there is so much about ancient Greece that we do not know—but also seem somewhat indeterminate by design. What, for example, are we to believe more—that the chorus of Lydian women (the willing *Bakkhai* rather than the forced, crazed *Bakkhai* of the house of Kadmos) feel a benign and ecstatic adoration of Dionysos and see him as the creativity of life itself, *or* that they feel a murderous unmitigated anger at Pentheus and see Dionysos as the rightly unappeasable destroyer, *or* that they feel pity for Agauë when Dionysos feels only rage? Or all three? All of this linguistic and literary richness is found in a text that is not only incomplete and corrupted in many places by those who copied it over the centuries, but that also stands—as we see it—in uncertain relation to earlier lost literary works, to mythology, and to the actual practices of worship of Dionysos. (See Charles Segal's Introduction, pp. 6–18.) Furthermore, later Christian attitudes — toward a god of death and rebirth, a god who is a son of god, and human history in which a father-god intervenes — are inextricably already a part of many present-day readers' thinking, and these attitudes of ours color our understanding of the play in ways foreign to it because they so thoroughly color our *language*; after all, the everyday English that we speak is very Christianized in its figures of speech, its traditional symbols, and in the connotations of certain words. We think, for example, of what happened to the potent pre-Christian symbolism of wine when it became Christianized.

From this tangle of problems — which even if they can to some extent be formulated can never be completely solved — let us turn to some practical aspects of the translation. The vocabulary of Euripides' play is not especially large, but is sometimes very peculiar; and, as I mentioned, some words are repeated or turned with telling effect, either reinforcing a meaning, or undercutting it with irony, or echoing earlier meaning in a new way. In this translation, I have tried to approximate at least some of these patterns of repetition, although in English, unfortunately, it happens that for some of the frequently used Greek words, the English equivalents (like wretched or miserable) are lumpy and lack pathos.

In the Greek, Dionysos, the chorus, and the mortal characters use language differently from each other and differently at different moments (when Agaue, for example, returns to Thebes with her grisly trophy, she enters singing the lines of an ode that is completed in repartee with the chorus; but with her father, shortly afterward, her dialogue is spoken). To try to suggest such differences, I have varied both the diction and the meter of the translation. In Greek all the choral odes were chanted or sung; the dialogue was apparently performed as speech — but presumably very performed, nevertheless. But, as I shall explain, the effect in English is inevitably flattened out, for reasons having to do with the poetic and linguistic resources of English itself, which are fewer than those of ancient Greek.

This may be the best place for me to note for readers new to ancient Greek drama a few aspects that affect how we should read even a translation of those works. In Greek performance, three male actors played all the principal roles (including those of female characters); the chorus also was male, and when representing women also wore women's clothing; all the actors wore masks, which included hair. On stage, all the playing of women's roles was a male imagining and performing of female experience — speech, song, and act — and in the audience, the response to this performance was also entirely or almost entirely male, for just as there were no women on stage, there may

have been none in the audience. The existing styles and forms of poems and performance that the dramatists used in order to construct the
large structure of the drama had been devised earlier for smaller audiences and more intimate spaces. But the audiences attending the
dramas could be very large, and the theaters were outdoors, so even
when and where the acoustics were best, I imagine that the actors must
have needed to produce a kind of stylized shouting for the dialogue;
the chanting and song may also have relied on powerful artificiality of
emphasis and effect in order to be heard. Add all these circumstances
to the peculiar language of the plays, found nowhere else in Greek
life, and the problem of translation becomes so steeped in cultural
difference that it is no wonder that most translations are, as much as
anything else, simply evidence of the difficulty—and on some level the
impossibility—of the task. It's no surprise that translations of ancient
Greek drama often seem to sound strange when we have the feeling
that perhaps they should sound familiar, and familiar when they should
sound strange.

Even if my command of ancient Greek were adequate for me to
understand well the meters of the verse and the effects of chanting and
singing on the sounds of the lines, these cannot be represented well
in English, because, first, the linguistic compression of the Greek is
impossible to reproduce in idiomatic English, and, second, the poetic
resources of English are smaller than those of Greek not only in terms
of the formal resources available to the poet but also in an audience's
knowledge of and responsiveness to verse forms and poetic structures.
Although ancient Greek makes frequent expressive use of the sounds
of words—with alliteration, repetition, and rhythm—it does not rhyme.
I have not rhymed the translation, either (except in the very last lines,
a perhaps sententious little tagged-on poem addressed to the audience
as a way to mark the ending), although rhyming in English could be
defended as a strategy for formalizing and complicating the English
somewhat. Instead, I have tried to create a certain irregular intensity of
the sounds of the words in English, where appropriate.

Furthermore, the dramatic resources of our contemporary stage,
while very nearly infinite in theory, seem smallest in practice precisely
where tragedy in an ancient Greek style would need them: in deliberately artificial, stagey chanting and singing of lines that would have
to be, in some serious way, different from any imaginable American
musical, yet not nearly as elaborate nor as removed from our popular
culture as is opera. Spectacle, such an overpowering aspect of nearly
all our contemporary entertainment, was not at all an important ele-
ment of ancient Greek drama, as this play shows. Instead, playwright

and actors and audience were all absorbed in the wonderfully vivid descriptions that the messengers give of what has happened elsewhere.

Even assuming that, to some readers and listeners, lines of metrical verse in English do still convey rhythmical nuances and qualifications of meaning (and rhythmical pleasure), there is no way in English to represent the sound of the rich variety of meters and song of the original. Greek poetry used pitch and stress and the variety of metrical feet as well as the variation in pattern and length of the poetic line, whereas traditional English poetry is far less flexible, and works by establishing one dominant meter and varying the rhythms of speech stress within it, without often varying the length of the line. So, once a meter is established in the opening lines of a poem in English, the foot does not normally change except by certain minor, accepted, occasional substitutions that simply add to the pleasures of linguistic rhythm and allow the poet some expressive wiggle-room within the scheme. This is especially true of the meter that predominates historically in verse in English, which is iambic. To clarify this difference with ancient Greek: the Greek odes mix various kinds of feet in lines of various length, whereas an English poem may but often won't vary the length of the line, and all the feet will be the same (most often, iambic). Meter in English gets its wonderful subtlety and liveliness from playing the infinite variety of the *rhythmic possibilities* of natural *speech* with and against the expected but not compulsory *unvarying pattern* of the way *meter* regularizes those rhythms.

As I have mentioned, ancient Greek, a highly inflected language, can cram far more meaning into a few words than can English. So, while it seemed the most natural thing in this translation to use a (sometimes loose) iambic meter for the *dialogue*, I have often needed more *feet* than five, the customary length of an English iambic line, and so I have stretched the lines to six and seven and even eight feet in order to keep them single in those parts of the play (called the *stichomythia*) when the pace is fast and in Greek each character speaks only one line. I have used blank verse (unrhymed iambic pentameter) for the narrative and discursive *speeches*; but in this case—and again, because English needs more words than Greek to say the same thing— I have used not more feet but rather more *lines* than there are in the original in order to keep the rhythm of the speeches steady and authoritative. (The one exception is the speech by Dionysos, disguised as the Stranger, that begins at line 714, which is cast in lines of six feet instead of five, in order to represent a change in the Greek meter to a longer line—perhaps this metrical difference marks the peculiar circumstance that in this speech the god himself is a messenger recounting what has happened elsewhere, but he is not the usual mortal messenger.) In the *odes*, I have used a fairly free, but somewhat accentual measure, so as to try to catch the energy of the very beautiful original by composing a rhythmically syncopated sort of line, of varying length, which quickens or slows with the syntax. Beautiful in what way? In sound, in the compression of the syntax, in the striking figures of speech and in formal symmetry. The odes—sung and danced at those crucial moments in the play when the chorus performed them between scenes of dialogue—were composed so that each pair of stanzas, strophe and antistrophe, is formally congruent, having the same number of lines and similar metrical patterns; I have produced only analogous, not exact, symmetries in the translation, although of course I have followed the Greek ode's presentation in these *formally similar* stanzas of *substantively different* and contrasting emphases.

A FEW SPECIFIC WORDS

For the sake of the foreignness, the very Greekness, of *Bakkhai*—the ancient Greek language, Greek beliefs and attitudes, and the Greek performance of poetry—I decided to de-Latinize the proper nouns, despite the classicists' convention of using a Latin name for the play (*Bacchae*) and Latin names (Bacchus, Cithaeron, etc.) for characters and place names. The Latin overlay seems to me to put another screen between us, as common readers rather than classicists, and the Greekness, and thus to tame some of the sheer strangeness of what was Greek.

But I have had to depart from my own rule in using some proper names and Greek words that are already so well-known in English by a conventional Latinized and Anglicized pronunciation that is not very like the Greek (Cyprus, Acheron, Hades, etc.) that I have assumed the reader might be distracted by having to pronounce them in any other way. (Translation is much like politics in the necessity of compromise; in fact, translation is very much politics of a cultural kind.) I also want to make note of the following Greek words, some of which are untranslatable:

HYBRIS: Instead of using *hubris* for this particular key word, I have used various phrases, different in different contexts, mostly to avoid using a word that, although it now exists in English, does not mean what the Greek original meant. The original term conveys in Greek a sense of violent mistreatment, of violation and insult, of affront to dignity and honor, of insolence, offense, outrage, and overstepping the bounds of what is proper.

THYRSOS: (plural: *thyrsoi*, pronounced *thür-soss, thür-soy*): This was a light staff made from a stalk of fennel to which some ivy was fastened at the top. I have sometimes left the word in this transliterated form, and at other times translated it (or another Greek word for it) as staff or rod. It has a curiously double significance in suggesting both male and female—aside from its obvious symbolic relationship to the male phallus, it also suggests, in the ivy tendril with which it is crowned, the force of growth in nature; and when the thyrsos is used by women as a weapon, Euripides also contrasts this delicate, light object, completely from nature, with what it can and does defeat— the heavy, forged iron and bronze spears of the settled world and of male warriors.

THIASOS: I have translated it variously, often as troupe; it is a band of the women who are celebrants or worshipers of Dionysos, called Bakkhantes or Bakkhai (pronounced *backh*-eye, with an aspirated *kh*), after one of the god's other names, Bakkhos. In this translation, the Bakkhantes are called the Bakkhai, throughout. (This one awkward transliteration seemed enough. I also used maenads [pronounced *mee*-nads], a familiar Latin word that seems unavoidable because it is already familiar to us in this form, which is in fact the Latin transliteration of another Greek name for the *Bakkhai*, the Greek *mainades*; this word in Greek means women who are mad, raving or frantic.) In addition to Bakkhos, Dionysos (a name that in Greek would have been pronounced something like "dee-oh-*nü*-soss," with the second syllable uttered at a higher pitch, and the *d* perhaps pronounced like our voiced *th*) has several other names, used at different moments by Euripides either to bring the particular significance of one of the names into play where it is relevant or to fit the Greek meter. Bromios (pronounced *brome*-ee-oss), suggests thundering or roaring. Euios (pronounced *eh*-ooh-ih-*oss*), is related to the cry *Euhoi!* (pronounced eh-ooh-*hoy!*), used by the *thiasos* as an ecstatic exclamation. The name Iakkhos also suggests an ecstatic shout. Another exclamation of the *thiasos* is Io! (pronounced ee-*oh*)— this is used by Dionysos and the Bakkhai as an expression of joy, fear, sorrow, or alarm, to call each other. Zeus is said in the play to call Dionysos *Dithyrambos* (pronounced dithür-*am*-boss), which associates Dionysos both with poetry (see our word dithyramb) and with a pun in Greek on his having been born twice—once from Sémelê and again from Zeus's thigh, neither birth having been natural, since Sémelê was killed by Zeus's lightning when she was still carrying her child. I have translated other Greek interjections as *Oh* or *Ah* or even *Aiee*, rather than such outdated interjections as *Alas*. Only Dionysos and the chorus of Bakkhai utter the unusual *Aah!*

The pronunciation of the names of the main characters, and a few who are only mentioned, are Agauë (ah-*gau*-eh; some translators Latinize this name to Agave); Ekhíon (eh-kh*ee*-on), the father of Pentheus; Ino (*ee*-no), sister of Agauë, thus another daughter of Kadmos, along with Autonoë (au-*ton*-oh-ee—the *ton* rhyming with our preposition on); Kadmos (*kad*-moss); Pentheus (*penth*-ee-us); Sémelê (*seh*-mel-eh), mortal mother of Dionysos; and Teiresias (Ty-*rees*-ee-ahss is our contemporary pronunciation of his well-known name); the earlier death of Autonoë's son Aktáion (ack-*tie*-on) is a prefiguring of the fate of his cousin Pentheus. Here and in the text of the play, the diacritical marks (accents and diaeresis) are *not* those of the Greek but are intended to aid pronunciation in English.

See the notes by Charles Segal for comments on the group of key Greek words having to do with mind and attitude that I have translated with such variations as wise, of sound mind, self-controlled, clever, smart, of good sense.

ACKNOWLEDGMENTS

I am most grateful to Charles Segal for his help with this translation; his counsel has been unfailingly wise, learned and friendly. For the extraodinary opportunity to work with him on this project, I am thankful to Oxford University Press and the coeditors of this series, Alan Shapiro and Peter Burian. The reader of this new version of Euripides in our own language and our own time should attribute any failure of ear or inventiveness to me.

Evanston, Illinois
April 2000

REGINALD GIBBONS

BAKKHAI

CHARACTERS

DIONYSOS the god, who except at the beginning and the end of the play appears in the mortal form of his disguise, the STRANGER. Also called BROMIOS (the Thunderer or Roarer), BAKKHOS, IAKKHOS (a name suggesting his holy cry or shriek), and EUIOS (suggesting a cry of joy)

CHORUS OF BAKKHAI women from Lydia, in Asia Minor, who as worshipers of Dionysos have accompanied him to Greece

TEIRESIAS the elderly blind soothsayer

KADMOS elderly founder of Thebes (a small Bronze Age city), who was formerly the head of the royal household of Thebes

PENTHEUS grandson of Kadmos; about eighteen or twenty years old

TWO MESSENGERS

VARIOUS ATTENDANTS (servants, guards)

AGAUË daughter of Kadmos and mother of Pentheus

Line numbers in the right-hand margin of the text refer to the English translation only, and the Notes on the text at p. 99 are keyed to these lines. The bracketed line numbers in the running head lines refer to the Greek text.

DIONYSOS *the god enters, alone, and stands before simple architectural shapes representing the tall royal house of Thebes, the adjacent monument to his dead mother,* SÉMELÊ, *and the ruin of her house, destroyed perhaps twenty-five or thirty years before, at* DIONYSOS' *birth. From the ruin smoke is still rising.*

DIONYSOS I, son of Zeus, have come to Theban soil —   1
           I, Dionysos, to whom Sémelê,
           Kadmos' daughter, gave a fiery birth
           When flames of lightning burst to bring me forth.
           Having changed my shape from god to mortal,
           Now I have come to where two rivers flow —
           The waters of the Dirkê and the Isménos.
           I see beside the royal house the tomb
           Of Sémelê, my mother, lightning-struck;
           And here's her ruined house still smoldering   10
           With the live flame of Zeus — the immortal rage
           And violence of Hera against my mother.
               But Kadmos I praise — he set aside this precinct
           As sacred to his daughter's memory.
           And then I covered it all around with vines
           Of wide green leaves and clusters of the grape.
               Leaving the country of the Phrygians,
           And the Lydians, rich in bright gold, and going
           Up to the heights of Persian plains, hard beaten
           By the sun, then onward to the high-walled towns   20
           Of the Baktrians, the grim hard lands of the Medes,
           To opulent Arabia and all
           Of Asia Minor, where in fine tall-towered
           Cities by the salt sea, barbarians
           And Greeks all mix together, I have come
           First to this city, here among the Greeks,
           After I set everyone in Asia
           Dancing and founded my rites there, so that
           All mortals would see that I am a god.
           It was Thebes, in all of Greece, that I made   30
           the first to raise the women's ecstatic cry.
           I clothed Thebes in the fawn skin, and I gave

Into its hand the thyrsos, too—the ivyJavelin—because
    my mother's sisters,
Who should have been the last, and the least inclined,
To deny me, did just that: denied that I
Am Dionysos, the son of Zeus. They said
That Sémelê had been taken by a man
And that she only claimed it was Zeus who was
To blame for the wrongdoing in her bed—   40
They thought this claim the sophistry of Kadmos.
My mother's sisters gloated to everyone
That this lie was the reason Zeus had killed her.
So, like a gadfly I have stung these sisters
To a frenzy, out of their very homes, to live
Crazed in the mountains. And I made them wear
The trappings of their service to me, also.
The whole female seed of Kadmos' kin,
Every woman of that family,
I've driven from their homes in a state of madness,   50
And now, together with my mother's sisters,
They sit on rocks, without a roof, beneath
The pale green pines. For Thebes must fully learn—
Despite itself, if need be, what neglect
Of my Bakkhic rituals means. And I, revealed
To mortals as the god she bore to Zeus,
Must speak in defense of Sémelê, my mother.
      Kadmos has handed all authority
Of rule to Pentheus, his daughter's son,
Who is at war with deity itself   60
When he behaves toward me as he does—
He is excluding me from his libations,
Making no mention of me when publicly
He calls upon the gods. But I will show
To him and Thebes that I was born a god.
When I've set this place to rights, I'll travel
To yet another country, to reveal
Myself again. And if this Theban city
Angrily takes up weapons and tries by force
To bring the Bakkhai down from the mountainside,   70
I will lead the maenads into battle—
That is why I've taken mortal shape,
Changed form to what in nature is a man.

Now the CHORUS *begin to file on stage from one side; they
do not hear what* DIONYSOS *is saying; some of the chorus
carry drums like large tambourines and others carry thyrsoi.*

And you, my sisterhood of worshipers,
Who left Mount Tmolos, fortress of Lydia,
You whom I brought from among barbarians
To sit beside me and share my wanderings,
Now you must beat your drums—the Phrygian drums
Invented by Mother Rhea and by me!
Surround this royal house of Pentheus   80
And beat the drums, so Kadmos' city hears!
I will go up the canyons of Mount Kitháiron,
To where the Bakkhai are, and join their dance.

DIONYSOS *exits. Throughout the play, some of the lines
sung or spoken by the chorus are uttered by all together,
others only by the chorus leader or other members of the
chorus; during the odes, as the chorus sing, they also
dance.*

CHORUS   *Parode (opening ode)*
                                                With accompanying drums.

Asia I left, sacred
Tmolos I left behind me,
        And for Bromios I race to sweet toil
        And weariness that is no toil nor weariness,
And I cry out in praise of the Bakkhic God—
        Who's standing in the road?
Who's in the way? Who's   90
In the great house? Move aside! Come out!
Let everyone keep mouths pure
        In holy silence!
For I will always sing in praise of Dionysos
The hymns that tradition says are his:

        O   *strophe*
        Blessed, truly happy is he
        Who knows the rituals
        Of the god, who joins his spirit

With the holy worshipers in the mountains,   100
Who through the holy purifying rites
Becomes one of the Bakkhai
And in the one right way celebrates
The mysteries of our great mother Kybélê
And swings the thyrsos high
Overhead and wears a crown
Of ivy and serves Dionysos!

Onward, Bakkhai! Onward, Bakkhai! —
Leading Bromios, god and child of god,
Dionysos, home from the mountains of Phrygia   110
To these Greek streets, broad
Streets for dancing, broad
    Greek streets, Bromios!

O   *antistrophe*
Dionysos! — who once lay curled
Within his mother in her pangs of childbirth
When to earth flew the lightning of Zeus
And at his thunderclap she thrust
The child too early from
Her womb and left this life.   120
Then instantly Zeus the son of Kronos
Took the infant into his own thigh,
Where he covered him and closed
With golden pins this chamber
Of a womb hidden away from Hera's sight.

When the Fates measured out
The term, then Zeus himself gave
Birth to the god with the horns of a bull,
And crowned him with a crown of snakes —
Which is why the maenads catch these eaters of   130
    What is wild and braid them through their hair.

Crown yourself with ivy,   *strophe*
O Thebes where Sémelê lived!
Abound, abound in
    Evergreen
Leaves and red berries, consecrate
Yourselves as Bakkhai with

Sprays of oak and pine!
Over your dappled fawn skins drape
White woolen curls and strands,   140
And with all your violent fennel-rods
    Be holy! Now the whole earth
    Will dance together when Bromios leads
Worshipers to the mountain, to the mountain—
Where the throng of women
Wait together, stung to a frenzy and driven
Away from their shuttles
And looms by Dionysos!

O chamber of the Koúretês,   *antistrophe*
O sacred reaches of island Crete!—   150
Where, in the cave of the birth
    Of Zeus
Triple-crested Korybantës
Devised for me
The circle of stretched hide!
In the frenzy of the dance
They joined this beat with the sweet
Calling breath of Phrygian
    Pipes, they gave the drum,
    Pounding for the Bakkhic cries   160
Of ecstasy, to Mother Rhea.
From her, the Mother Goddess,
Ecstatic satyrs took it
To the festivals where every other year
Our Dionysos rejoices when everyone is dancing.

How sweet he is in the mountains,   *epode*
When running with his worshipers he throws
Himself to the ground, wearing his holy fawn skin—
Rapture of killing and the spilled
    Blood, of eating   170
Raw the flesh of the hunted goat!
Racing across the mountains of Phrygia, of Lydia!
    Bromios leads us!
Euhói!
From the earth comes flowing milk, flowing
Wine, flowing nectar of bees! The Bakkhic One
Lifts his blazing torch high,

The sweet pine smoke streams
Like Syrian frankincense as he races
    Holding the staff of fennel—   180
    Running and dancing, joyously
    Crying, Dionysos stirs
    The straggling maenads to shake
    With rapture and he whips
His long fine hair in the air of heaven.
    Amidst their joyful cries
    He roars to them, "Onward,
    Bakkhai! Onward, Bakkhai!
    You are the pride of gold-
    Giving Mount Tmolos,   190
Sing of Dionysos to the thundering drumbeats,
Your shouts of rapture exalt
The god of joyful cry
With Phrygian crying and calling,
When the melodious holy
Pipes with holy notes
Resound around those
Who throng to the mountain,
    To the mountain!"
Then, like a joyful foal, when it plays   200
Near the grazing mare, the woman
Worshiper swiftly, nimbly leaps!

SCENE I

TEIRESIAS *enters—an old man moving feebly.*

TEIRESIAS Who's there at the gate? Call Kadmos from the house—
    Agénor's son, who left his city, Sidon,
    Came here and built these towers of Thebes. Go in,
    Someone, say that Teiresias has come
    To see him. He knows why I'm here, and what
    Agreement I have with him—of one old man
    With an older one—to craft our thyrsoi, wear
    Fawn skins, and crown our heads with ivy tendrils.   210

KADMOS *emerges from the royal house—also old*
and moving feebly.

KADMOS   Ah, my dear friend!—I recognized your voice
         From inside my house as soon as I could hear you—
         It's a wise man's wise voice. And now I'm ready!
         I have put on these trappings of the god.
         For he's my daughter's child, our Dionysos,
         A god revealed to mortals, whom we must
         Magnify in any way we can.
         So where do we go now to dance? And what
         Are the steps our feet must learn? Where do we toss
         These old gray heads? Explain, Teiresias,   220
         Tell me as one old man to another—you
         Are the wise one. And I won't weary, not
         In the least, pounding my thyrsos on the earth
         All day and all night, too—and what a joy
         To forget that we are old!

TEIRESIAS   Then you feel just
         As I do—young! I'll try to dance the dance.

KADMOS   Do we go up the mountain by chariot?

TEIRESIAS No—that would not honor the god as much.

KADMOS   Shall one old man lead the other like a child to school?

TEIRESIAS The god will lead us effortlessly to himself.   230

KADMOS   Are we the only ones in Thebes to dance for Bakkhos?

TEIRESIAS Yes—only we have any sense, the rest have none.

KADMOS   We have delayed too long, now. Take my hand.

TEIRESIAS See, then—join hands with me, make two hands one.

KADMOS   I don't despise the gods—am I not mortal?

TEIRESIAS In matters of the gods, we don't engage
         In sophistries. Traditions of our fathers,
         Which we received when time began, cannot
         Be overthrown by argument, not even
         By the utmost thought that sometimes reaches wisdom.   240

51

KADMOS Because I want to dance and wear a crown
Of ivy, will some person say I show
No respect for my old age?

TEIRESIAS   Not so. The god
Makes no distinction between the young and old
When men are called to celebrate his dance.
He wishes to be honored and exalted
By all alike, and no one is excluded.

KADMOS Since you can't see this light, Teiresias,
I will interpret for you with my words:
Here's Pentheus—he's striding, filled with zeal,   250
Toward the house—Ekhíon's child, to whom
I gave the power to rule this soil. But how
Flustered he is! What new wild thing will he say?

With a few ATTENDANTS, PENTHEUS *enters, very agitated.*

PENTHEUS Just when I happen to be outside this land,
What do I hear? New evils! Women leave
Our houses for bogus revels ("Bakkhic" indeed!),
Dashing through the dark shade of mountain forests
To honor with their dancing this new god,
Dionysos—whoever he may be—
And right in their midst they set full bowls of wine,   260
And slink into the thickets to meet men there,
Saying they are maenads sacrificing,
When really they rank Aphrodite first,
Over Bakkhos! I've caught and shackled some
By the hands, in city prisons, under guard,
And those at large, I'll hunt down on the mountain:
[Ino, and Agauë—who by Ekhíon
Gave birth to me—and Autonoë, the mother
Of Aktáion.] I'll bind them up in nets of iron
And stop their evil Bakkhic revels fast.   270
People say some stranger has arrived,
A sorcerer, a Lydian casting spells,
His long blond hair perfumed, his cheeks as red
As wine, his eyes with the charm of Aphrodite's.
And all day long and all night, too, they say,

52

He mingles with young girls, he promises them
His mysteries of joyous rapture—but
If I catch him around here, within our borders,
I'll stop him pounding with his thyrsos and tossing
His hair—for through his throat I'll cut his head   280
Off of his body. *He* says Dionysos
Is a god, *he* says Dionysos was
Sewn into the thigh of Zeus! But Dionysos
Was burnt up with his mother by the flame
Of the lightning bolt—because she lied about
Her marriage-bed with Zeus. Such terrible things—
Don't they deserve hanging, as outrages
Beyond outrage, whoever this stranger is?

PENTHEUS *notices the two old men.*

But here's Teiresias, the prophet, dressed
In dappled fawn skins! Yet another wonder!   290
And mother's father—how ridiculous!—
Reveling like the Bakkhai with his thyrsos!
Sir, I reject the sight of you like this—
Old age without a shred of sense. Won't you
Shake that ivy off and drop that thyrsos,
Father of my mother? Teiresias,
You talked him into this—you introduce
Yet another god to mortals so
You can interpret the omens of birds and make
People pay you at burnt offerings.   300
If your white hair did not protect you, you
Would be imprisoned, held with all the Bakkhai
For having brought these sinister mystic rites
Among us here—for when the women have
The bright grape-cluster gleaming at their feasts,
There's nothing healthy in these rites, I say.

CHORUS What sacrilege! Irreverence! O stranger,
Do you not revere the gods and Kadmos—
Who planted the crop of earth-born men? Will you,
Ekhíon's child, bring shame on all your kin?   310

TEIRESIAS It's no great task to speak well, when a man's
Intelligent and starts well with good words.

53

But you: your tongue runs smoothly, as if you had
Some understanding. Yet your words are senseless.
A man like you, whose strength is that he's bold,
Who's good at speaking, too, can only make
A bad citizen—for he lacks good sense.
As for this new god whom you mock with laughter—
The greatness he will have in Greece surpasses
My power to explain. Listen to me,   320
Young man—there are two great first things that we
As mortals have: the goddess of the Earth,
Deméter—call her by whatever name
You wish—gave us our solid food, and he
Who came next, Sémelê's child, gave us liquid—
From the grape—as counterpart to Deméter's bread.
The god's invention, it gives us poor mortals
Release from pain and sorrow, when we're filled
With what flows from the vine; it gives us sleep,
When we can forget the evils of the day.   330
Nor for us mortals can another drug
For suffering surpass it. Himself a god,
He is poured out to the other gods, so that
From him we mortals have what's good in life.
And you—you laugh and mock him for his birth
From Zeus's thigh? I'll teach you the excellence
Of this: When Zeus snatched Dionysos up
From the flames of his own thunderbolt, and brought
The infant to Olympos as a god,
Hera would have hurled the child from heaven.   340
But Zeus, opposing her, devised his scheme—
One such as only a god could ever form:
He broke away a *limb* of the body of air,
The aether that surrounds the earth on *high*.
He gave this limb to Hera to pacify her,
Thus saving Dionysos. Later, when mortals
Said that the god was stitched in Zeus's *limb*,
His *thigh*, they changed the *high* to *thigh* (because
On *high* the god was hostage to a goddess)
And told the story to fit the change of words.   350
        This god is also prophet: there's mantic power
In both the Bakkhic and the crazed—for when
The god completely fills the body, those
He maddens tell the future. He has his share

Of Ares, too—for soldiers, fully armed,
Drawn up in battle ranks, may fly in fright
Before they've even touched their spears: this too
Is madness put in men by Dionysos.
    And you will see him leaping on the heights
Of Delphi, some day, torch-flame in his hand,   360
Brandishing the Bakkhic staff, up there
On the high plateau between the two tall peaks,
And great through all of Greece. So Pentheus,
Believe me—do not boast that mortal rule
Masters men, nor think that you are wise,
When thinking, the way you do it, is diseased.
Welcome the god within this land and pour
Libations, crown your head and join the Bakkhai.
    It's not for Dionysos to compel
Women to modesty and self-control   370
In matters of Aphrodite, for modesty
With respect to everything lies in their nature.
Consider that even in the Bakkhic revels
A woman of true self-control will not
Be corrupted. Do you see this? You rejoice
When shouting hordes stand at the city gates
To give honor to the name of Pentheus—
I think that Dionysos, too, enjoys
The pleasure of acclaim. So I—and Kadmos,
Despite your mocking him—will crown our heads   380
With ivy and will dance. A gray-haired pair,
Yes. But we must dance, even so. And you
Will not persuade me with your words to fight
Against divinity. You are acting most
Painfully mad. No drug can cure your sickness
When it seems some drug has made you sick.

CHORUS Old man, with such good words you do not shame
       Apollo.
  Your praise for Bromios shows your wise good sense.

KADMOS My boy, Teiresias has said to you
  Only what he should say. Live as we do,   390
  And not beyond the order of the laws.
  Right now you are extremely flustered, so
  Your thinking makes no sense. And even if

This is not the god, consider him
A god and call him such. And tell a lie
For a good cause—that he is Sémelê's son—
So it will seem she gave birth to a god,
And all our clan is honored. You know how
Aktáion ended: female hounds, the eaters
Of raw flesh, dogs that he had raised, tore him   400
Apart: and this was his sad fate for boasting
In mountain meadows that he was a hunter
Greater than Artemis! May you not suffer
This! Come, let me crown your head with ivy.
Join us in giving to the god full honor.

PENTHEUS Let go of me! Off to your Bakkhic rites!
Don't smear your stupid folly onto me!
I'll punish him who taught you to be foolish.

To his ATTENDANTS.

Quickly, go where this man has his seat
For interpreting the meaning of bird song—   410
Pry it apart with bars and tear it down,
Pile everything together in one heap,
Throw his holy ribbands to the wind
And rain. With this one deed, I'll bite him hardest.
The rest of you, search Thebes until you find
This stranger who looks female, who has brought
A new disease that sickens all our women,
And who corrupts their beds! And if you find him,
Bind him and bring him here, so that he may
Receive his justice: death by stoning—after   420
He sees a bitter Bakkhic revel in Thebes!

TEIRESIAS You stubborn man, how ignorant you are
Of what you're saying! Earlier, you acted
Crazy enough, but now you're truly mad.
Kadmos, for his sake—savage though he is—
And for the city's sake, let's go to plead
That the god do nothing unusual.
Come with me, and bring your ivy staff,
Help me stay on my feet, and I will do
The same for you—it would bring shame on us   430

If we two elders fell, but go we must.
We must be slaves to Bakkhos, son of Zeus.
May Pentheus not make your house repent,
Kadmos. I say this not to prophesy—
The fact is there: the fool speaks foolish things.

*After their brief moment of youthful liveliness and then
their argument with* PENTHEUS, TEIRESIAS *and* KADMOS
exit, moving shakily again; PENTHEUS *goes into the royal
house.*

The CHORUS *dance and sing*

CHORUS   *First stasimon (second ode)*
    O Lady Holiness,   *strophe*
    Revered among the gods,
    O Holiness, you
    Who on golden wings
    Pass soaring above the earth—   440
    Do you hear these words
    Of Pentheus? Do you hear
    His wrong, impure, unholy
    Insults against Bromios,
        Sémelê's son, the first-blessed god
        At the festive banquets crowned with
        Lovely garlands of flowers and ivy?—
    The god whose part, there, is
    To join the dancing worshipers,
    To laugh with the notes of the pipe,   450
    To end our worries when
    The gleaming grape-cluster arrives
    At our great feast in celebration
    Of the gods and when
        Amidst the ivied feasts the wine-
        Bowl wraps sleep around all the men.

    Mouths unbridled and   *antistrophe*
    Folly flaunting the law
    End in misfortune,
    But a life of calm   460
    And of wise thinking

Will not be
Wrecked by storms,
And will keep
The household safe and whole.
        For even though the gods dwell so far
        Away in the air of heaven, they
        See what mortals do.
Intellect is not wisdom.
And to think in a manner   470
Not right for mortals means
Life will be short. Who
Would pursue great things
If doing so meant losing what
Is already his?
        That is the way, as I see it,
        And bad counsel, of madmen.

O let me go to Cyprus,   *strophe*
Island of great Aphrodite,
To Paphos where gods of desire   480
        Cast a spell on the mortal mind—
Blooming Paphos luxuriantly
Fruitful with the waters of
The wide barbarian rainless
River of a hundred mouths—
And to Pieria, most beautiful
Habitation of the Muses
Where sacred Mount Olympos
Slopes gravely downward—
Lead me there, Bromios!   490
Bromios, god of ecstatic
Cry who guides the Bakkhai!
There we will find the Graces,
There we'll find Desire,
There the very law is
        To celebrate your mysteries!

Our god, the son of Zeus,   *antistrophe*
Rejoices in festivities
And loves the goddess Peace—who gives us
        Our plenty and rears our children.   500

To the rich and the poor alike
Our god has given
The delight of wine, that frees us
From our grief, and he hates
Anyone who does not
Want to live, both by day
And by precious night, a life
Of blessed happiness, and
Anyone who does not want to
Keep a wise heart   510
And a wise mind safe
From arrogant men.
Whatever everyone, all
Simple, ordinary people,
        Prefer and do, this I accept.

SCENE II

PENTHEUS *enters again from the royal house, converging
with* GUARDS *entering from offstage, two of whom are holding between them, by the arms, the* STRANGER, *whose
hands are bound.*

GUARD Here we arc, Pentheus! We've hunted down
        The prey, the one you sent us out to catch—
        Our search was not in vain. We found this beast
        Was gentle, and he didn't run, but held out
        His hands to us, he didn't even pale,   520
        His cheeks stayed flushed with wine, he laughed and said
        To bind his hands and lead him off—he waited
        To make that job quite easy for us. I was
        Ashamed. I said, "Stranger, I don't arrest you
        Because I want to, but because I was sent
        By Pentheus, who ordered me to do it."
            As for the Bakkhai you locked up, the ones
        You took away and bound and shackled in chains
        In the town prison—now they're gone! Set free!
        They're running away towards the mountain clearings,   530
        Leaping and calling on their Dionysos
        As a god. Their ankle-chains just fell away

59

By themselves, the doors no mortal hand had touched
Swung wide open, unbolted. Full of wonders,
This man has come to Thebes!—but whatever is
To happen next is your concern, not mine.

PENTHEUS Untie his hands. He's in my net, he won't
              Escape me now. Well, you do have the shape
              Of a man whose body women don't find ugly.
              Isn't that just what you came here for?   540
              Your hair is much too long to be a wrestler's,
              Flowing down to your cheeks that way, and full
              Of lust. You've kept your skin quite fair, by staying
              Out of the sun, and well in the shade, to hunt
              For Aphrodite, pretty as you are.
              First, tell me of your home, your family.

DIONYSOS I will tell you readily—it's easy.
              You've heard of Mount Tmolos, thick with flowers?

PENTHEUS Yes, it makes a circle around the town of Sardis.

DIONYSOS I am from there—my country's Lydia.   550

PENTHEUS These rites you bring to Greece—where are they from?

DIONYSOS Dionysos himself, the son of Zeus, initiated me.

PENTHEUS Some Zeus from over there, who begets new gods?

DIONYSOS None but the Zeus who yoked Sémelê to himself, here.

PENTHEUS Were you compelled by him in dreams, or awake in
              daylight?

DIONYSOS Face to face—and he gives me mystic rites.

PENTHEUS These mystic rites of yours—what are they like?

DIONYSOS They must not be known by mortals who aren't Bakkhai.

PENTHEUS How do they benefit the ones who make the ritual
              sacrifice?

DIONYSOS That's not for you to hear—although it's worth your
             knowing.   560

PENTHEUS You counterfeit a good reply, so that I'll want to hear.

DIONYSOS The rites of the god would scathe a nonbeliever.

PENTHEUS The god—you claim you saw him clearly—what was he
             like?

DIONYSOS Whatever he wished—I did not order him about.

PENTHEUS How cleverly you channel this aside, and say not a thing!

DIONYSOS Wise things to the ignorant will sound like nonsense.

PENTHEUS Is Thebes the first place where you've brought the god?

DIONYSOS Among barbarians, these rites are danced by everyone.

PENTHEUS Because they have less sense than do we Greeks.

DIONYSOS In this, at least, they have good sense—but different
             customs.   570

PENTHEUS Do you perform the rites by day?—or night?

DIONYSOS Mostly at night—because the darkness has its holiness.

PENTHEUS It's treacherous, for women, and corrupts them.

DIONYSOS What's shameful can be found even by light of day.

PENTHEUS You must be punished for your evil sophistries.

DIONYSOS And you—for ignorance and lack of piety toward the god.

PENTHEUS What Bakkhic boldness! An acrobat of words!

DIONYSOS Tell me what I'll suffer. What terrible thing will you do
             to me?

PENTHEUS First I'll have that delicate hair cut off.

DIONYSOS My hair is sacred—I grow it for the god.   580

PENTHEUS Next, give up that thyrsos with your own hand.

DIONYSOS Take it from me yourself: I carry it for Dionysos.

PENTHEUS We will guard your body inside, in chains.

DIONYSOS The god himself will set me free, whenever I so wish.

PENTHEUS Yes—if you call him while standing with the maenads.

DIONYSOS He's right here, now, and sees what I am suffering.

PENTHEUS Where is he, then? My eyes don't see him here.

DIONYSOS He's where I am. Because of your irreverence you cannot
          see him.

PENTHEUS Hold this man. He scorns both me and Thebes.

DIONYSOS I tell all of you: don't bind me—I am sane and you are
          not.   590

PENTHEUS And I say: I rule you and they'll bind you.

DIONYSOS You don't know what your life is, nor what you're doing,
          nor who you are.

PENTHEUS I am Pentheus, Agauë's son, Ekhíon was my father.

DIONYSOS Your name means grief, and you are suited for it.

PENTHEUS Begone. Confine him to the horses' stalls
          So that he may see only gloom and darkness.
               You can do your dancing there. And these
          Women you've brought as your accomplices
          In evil, we'll either sell or—once I've stopped
          Their hands from beating on these drums—I'll own   600
          As household slaves working at looms, inside.

62

DIONYSOS I'm ready to go. What is not meant to be,
I won't have to suffer. But you! The god
In whose existence you do not believe,
Dionysos, will chase you down and then
Exact his compensation for your insults.
In putting us in chains, it's him you wrong.

> DIONYSUS *and* PENTHEUS *exit, with* GUARDS, *into the royal house.*

The CHORUS *dance and sing.*

CHORUS   *Second stasimon (third ode)*
O Lady Dírkê, river-   *strophe*
    Daughter of Akheloüs, blessed
Maiden — once, you took into   610
Your waters the infant of Zeus,
    When his father plucked that child
From the flames of his own
Immortal fire to hide
Him in his thigh, and cried out,
"Go, Dithyrambos, twice-born, into
My male womb. I reveal
You, Bakkhos, to Thebes,
To be called by this name."
But blessed Dírkê,   620
You push me away when I have
Filled your banks with ivy-crowned dancers.
Why do you reject me?
Why do you run from me?
    Someday, I swear
    By the joyful grape-clusters
    Of Dionysos' vine —
    Someday you won't be
Able to think of anything but Bromios.

Pentheus, the spawn   *antistrophe*   630
    Of earth itself, reveals
He is descended from
A dragon, fathered by earth-
    Born Ekhíon as a monster
With the face of a beast,

No mortal man but some
Savage murderous giant who
Battles the gods. And soon
He'll bind me with ropes because I
Belong to Bromios! Already   640
He holds in his house
My reveling companion, hidden
Away in dark prison.
Do you see this, Dionysos,
O son of Zeus?—that those
Who praise you are in bonds
        And must struggle against them? Come,
        Lord, come down from
        Olympos brandishing your thyrsos
        With its golden face!   650
End the insults of a murderous man!

Dionysos—where on Mount Nysa,   *epode*
The mother-nurse of all wild creatures,
Are you leading your worshipers with
Your thyrsos? Or are you atop
Korykian mountain peaks?
        Or perhaps in the dark thick forests of Olympos
        Where Orpheus playing his lyre gathered
Around him the listening trees,
Around him the listening beasts?   660
O much-blessed Mount Pieria,
Euios will make you sacred,
Dancing his revels with
His troupe of Bakkhai
Across the rushing River Axios
He'll come with the whirling maenads,
        And over the river Lydias, father
        Of fortune, giver of gladness—
Clearest waters of Lydias, I hear it said,
That fatten that realm of famed horses.   670

SCENE III

These lines are sung.

DIONYSOS

From within the royal house, in the god's voice.

Io!
Io Bakkhai! Io Bakkhai! Hear me, hear my voice!

CHORUS   Who's shouting? Who? And where's that cry from?
That shout of Euios that summons me!

DIONYSOS Io! Io! I call again, I --
Son of Sémelê, son of Zeus!

CHORUS   Io! Io! Master, master,
Come to your holy followers,
O Bromios! Bromios!

DIONYSOS Lady Earthquake, come shake the floor of the world!   680

CHORUS   Aaah! Aaah!
Pentheus' rafters will pitch till they tumble!
Dionysos is here in the halls!
Revere him in awe!
We do! We do!
Do you see at the top of the columns, the lintels of stone,
So high, that are breaking apart? ·
Thundering Bromios is shouting
His triumph from inside the house!

DIONYSOS Bring the torch burning to strike bright as lightning!   690
Burn and burn down the whole house of Pentheus!

CHORUS   Aaah! Aaah!
Do you see the fire? Do you see
Sémelê's holy tomb surrounded
By flames from the lightning that Zeus
Once hurled from heaven?
Throw yourselves down, maenads!
Throw your shaking bodies to the ground!

The Lord will come into this house
To pile it upside down in a heap—   700
The Lord, son of Zeus!

> *End of sung lines. Now* DIONYSOS *enters from the house,*
> *still disguised as the* STRANGER.

DIONYSOS   Barbarian women, are you so startled and so filled with
                    fear
           That you fall to the ground? What you seem to have felt
           Was the Bakkhic god shaking apart the house of
                    Pentheus.
           All of you rise up now and be brave and stop your
                    trembling.

CHORUS   O greatest light of the joyful cries of the Bakkhanal,
           What joy to see your face in my desolate loneliness!

DIONYSOS   Did you feel afraid when you saw them take me inside,
           Did you think I was cast into Pentheus' dark prison?

CHORUS   How could I not? If you met some disaster, who would
                    protect me?   710

           When you met that unholy man, how were you freed?

DIONYSOS   Easily I saved myself, without the slightest toil.

CHORUS   Didn't he tie your hands tightly with knotted ropes?

DIONYSOS   That's how I humbled and insulted him: he thought
           He had bound me, but never held and never touched
                    me—
           He only hoped he did. So when he led me in,
           His prisoner, to the manger, and he found a bull there,
           He bound its legs and hobbled its hooved feet, not mine.
           Breathing out his very spirit, he was dripping sweat,
           Biting his lips, as I sat near, completely calm,   720
           Watching him. And at that moment, Bakkhos entered,
           Shaking walls and striking fire at his mother's tomb.
           When Pentheus saw this, he thought his house was
                    burning
           And he rushed around and told his servants to bring water—

To bring the river Akheloüs itself! His slaves
Worked hard but all their labor was pointless and in vain.
Then he quit his toiling. Thinking that I had escaped,
He lifted a dark sword high and rushed into the house.
Now Bromios—it seems to me, at least, that this
Is what took place—now Bromios made a phantom shape   730
Hover in the courtyard and Pentheus chased after it,
He charged headlong at this shining air, stabbing it
       through
As if he thought that he could slaughter me. Beyond
All this, Bakkhos did more to him, to bring him low:
He shook the buildings down—the place has all
       collapsed.
So much for Pentheus. Bitterly he is staring
At the bonds he put on me. Exhausted, he has dropped
His sword and fallen down—for he dared battle against
A god, but he is only a man. And I came out
Quite calm, to you—without a thought of Pentheus.   740
Do I hear footsteps in the house? It seems to me
He'll come out, now. And after all that has happened,
       what
Can he say? But even if he still is blowing hard,
I will endure him easily, because a man
Who is wise has self-control and gentleness of temper.

> PENTHEUS *enters from the royal house—furious*
> *and "flustered."*

PENTHEUS   What terrible, strange things I've suffered, now!
      That foreigner I had just tied up escaped!
      Oh! Oh!
      There he is! What is this? How can you
      Appear outside, here in front of my house?   750

DIONYSOS   Slow your steps! Your temper needs a calm foundation!

PENTHEUS   How did you untie yourself and get out?

DIONYSOS   Didn't I say—or didn't you hear—that someone would set
      me free?

PENTHEUS   But who? You're always bringing in something strange.

DIONYSOS He who grows for me the vine of clustered grapes.

PENTHEUS For Dionysos, that boast is more reproach than praise.
I order the circle of walls and towers completely closed!

DIONYSOS What good will that do? Don't the gods leap walls?

PENTHEUS You're oh so smart, so smart except in what would count.

FIRST MESSENGER *enters as* DIONYSOS *is speaking*
the next line.

DIONYSOS Where it's needed, there of course I'm smart.   760
But now this man has come from the mountainside —
Listen to him and learn what he will tell.
We will wait — we will not run away.

FIRST MESSENGER Pentheus, you who rule this Theban ground,
I have just arrived from Mount Kitháiron,
Where glittering falls of brilliant snow still lie.

PENTHEUS What is it that you'd tell us with such zeal?

FIRST MESSENGER Seeing the sacred maenads, whose bare limbs
Moved swift as spears when they flashed away from
Thebes
Stung to a frenzy, I come here to tell you,   770
My lord — as I would tell the city, too —
That what they're doing now is strange, is greater
Than any wondrous miracle. I wish
To hear if I can speak freely of what
I saw — or do I need to trim my sails?
I'm afraid of how your thoughts will rush, my lord.
I fear your kingly temper and your power.

PENTHEUS Speak! For in any case you'll not be harmed
By me — one should not rage at those who are just.
The worse the things you say about the maenads,   780
The more I'll add to the punishment of him
Who introduced his wiles among the women.

68

FIRST MESSENGER When the sun's rays began to warm the earth,
                Our grazing herds of cattle were ascending
                Toward the high crags, and that was when I saw
                Three troupes of women: Autonoë was leader
                Of the first troupe, and then Agaüe herself—
                Your mother—was in charge of the second troupe,
                And Ino of the third. And all were sleeping—
                At their ease, some of them were lying down   790
                On soft pine needles, others on oak leaves,
                Resting their heads on the ground wherever they wished.
                And modestly. Not drunk—as you have said—
                From the wine bowl, nor to the tunes of the pipes
                Hunting one by one for sex in the woods.
                Your mother must have heard our cattle lowing,
                For she stood up with a drawn-out cry to wake
                The women, who threw their deep sleep from their eyes
                And rose quickly—a marvel of good order
                And good grace: women young and old, and girls   800
                Who have yet to be yoked in marriage. First
                They let their hair fall to their shoulders, then
                They tied their fawn pelts up—those that were loose—,
                Fastening the dappled skins with snakes
                That licked their cheeks. Some women cradled wild
                Gazelle kids and wolf cubs close in their arms
                To suckle them with their pale milk—because
                Those who have just given birth have left
                Their babies home and now their breasts are swollen.
                They crowned themselves with ivy, oak leaves, vines.   810
                One of them struck her thyrsos on a rock,
                From which a cold fresh stream of water leapt.
                Another touched her fennel-staff to earth,
                And up flowed springs of wine. And those who longed
                For milk began to dig by hand, and spurts
                Of it surged up. Honey began to pour
                From the ivied rods they carry. So, if you
                Had been there, too, and seen what I have seen,
                You'd pray to Dionysos rather than
                Condemn him . . .
                                 We began to argue, a bit—   820
                Cowherds and shepherds gathered to compare
                These strange, miraculous events—and one
                Of us, who used to wander through the town,

And was good at talking, said, "All of you who
Live on these sacred mountains: shall we hunt
Agaue, mother of lord Pentheus,
Take her from these Bakkhic revels, and gain
The master's favor?" This was a good idea,
We thought—and where they would come by, we hid
In thickets for an ambush.
                                 When it was time,   830
They raised their sacred staffs to begin their dances,
Calling together on Bromios as "Iakkhos,"
The son of Zeus. And all the mountain, all
The creatures of the wild, joined them till nothing
That lived was left outside the running dance.

Agaue happened to fling herself near me,
And I sprang out, leaving my hiding place,
To try to take good hold of her, but she
Called to them, "O hounds of the chase, these men
Are hunting us! Follow me! Follow me   840
Bearing not arms but thyrsoi as your weapons!"
We ran away from them—to escape being torn
Apart by the maenads. But with their bare hands,
Not with weapons of iron, then they began
To attack the grazing herds. You would have seen
One woman by herself with just her hands
Pulling in two a big young heifer that
Had swelling udders and was bellowing,
And meanwhile others were dismembering
The full-grown cattle, flaying them to shreds.   850
You would have seen the ribs and hooves hurled up,
Thrown down, flying through the air, and pieces
Hanging from the trees, still dripping blood.
Even arrogant bulls were stumbling, forced
To the ground, the anger in their horns outweighed
By the countless hands of girls—their rags of flesh
Were torn from them much faster than you could
Have blinked your royal eyes.
                                        And then like birds
They rose and sped across the spreading plains
Where Theban wheat grows thick beside the river—   860
On towns in Mount Kithairon's foothills they fell
Like enemies, and plundered Hysiái
And Erythrái, and turned them upside down.

They snatched the children of those towns from their
     homes,
And everything they carried on their shoulders
Stayed where they put it and never fell, without
Their even having tied it to themselves!
And in their hair they carried blazing fire,
Which did not burn them . . . People in the towns
Felt fury at this pillage and fought back.   870
And that, my lord, was an awful thing to see:
For men threw pointed spears and yet could draw
No blood, neither with bronze nor iron—instead,
The women, hurling thyrsoi with their hands,
Dealt those people many wounds, and made
Them turn their backs and run. Women defeated
The men—and not without some god.
                                        After that,
They returned to where they had departed from—
Those springs the god had given them. They washed
The blood away, and what was on their cheeks   880
The snakes cleaned off by licking . . .
                                   And so, O master,
Receive this god, whoever he may be,
Into our city, because his power is great—
Both in other matters and also, as I
Have heard them say, in this: it's he who gave
To mortals the vine that stops all suffering.
And if wine were to exist no longer, then
Neither would the goddess Aphrodite,
Nor anything of pleasure for us mortals.

CHORUS   I'm frightened to speak freely to the king,   890
         But even so, it must be said to him
         That Dionysos is beneath no god!

PENTHEUS Outrageous Bakkhic violence blazes up
          Close by like wildfire—and to Greeks this is
          An intolerable rebuke! I won't delay!
          Go to the Elektran Gate! And summon all
          Our troops!—bearers of heavy shields and riders
          Of swiftest horses, those who carry spears
          And those whose hands make bowstrings sing with arrows.

71

We go to war against the Bakkhai! This is   900
Too much to bear—that what we're made to suffer
We should suffer at the hands of women.

DIONYSOS Pentheus: you have heard me speak, but you
Do not do what I say. And even though
I've been mistreated by you, still I tell you
Not to raise arms against a god—be calm,
For Bromios will not let you force the Bakkhai
Down from the mountains that resound with joy.

PENTHEUS Will you stop lecturing me and—since you've escaped
your bonds—
Hold onto your freedom? Or I'll punish you again!   910

DIONYSOS I would sacrifice to him instead of kicking angrily
Against the pricking goads—mortal fighting a god.

PENTHEUS Sacrifice is just what I'll do, by slaughtering the women—
Who entirely deserve it, in those canyons on Mount
Kitháiron.

DIONYSOS You will be routed—and disgraced, that Bakkhai
With ivy rods should turn away bronze shields.

PENTHEUS There's no way forward, wrestling with this stranger,
Who won't be silent, whether suffering or free.

DIONYSOS And yet—my friend—it's possible to set things right.

PENTHEUS But how? Being a slave to those who are my slaves?   920

DIONYSOS I'll bring the women here, without one weapon.

PENTHEUS Undoubtedly some trick you play on me.

DIONYSOS What trick, if I by my devices wish to save you?

PENTHEUS You made a pact with them to be Bakkhai forever.

DIONYSOS Of that, be certain—but my pact is with the god.

PENTHEUS

To an ATTENDANT.

Fetch me my weapons!

to DIONYSOS:

You—be silent, now!

The ATTENDANT *leaves to bring* PENTHEUS *his weapons
from the royal house.* PENTHEUS *turns to follow him.*

DIONYSOS Aaah!

PENTHEUS stops and looks back at DIONYSOS, *and as they
speak, returns to him.*

Do you want to see them sitting together on the mountain?

PENTHEUS Yes, I do—for that, I'd give a countless weight of gold.

DIONYSOS But why do you feel such desire for this?   930

PENTHEUS It would pain me if I saw them drunk.

DIONYSOS And yet you'd see with pleasure that which gives you
              pain?

PENTHEUS Yes—sitting beneath the fir trees, without a sound.

DIONYSOS But they will track you down, even if you hide.

PENTHEUS A good point—so I'll go openly to them.

DIONYSOS Shall we lead you, then? Will you undertake the journey?

PENTHEUS Lead me fast as you can—this waiting irritates me.

DIONYSOS Put on the ritual robe of linen, then.

73

PENTHEUS What for? Am I, a male, supposed to rank myself as
          female?

DIONYSOS So they won't kill you if they see you're male.   940

PENTHEUS You're right, again. How smart you've always been.

DIONYSOS It was Dionysos who taught us these things so well.

PENTHEUS What should I do to follow your advice?

DIONYSOS I'll go inside the house and dress you there.

PENTHEUS In what dress? Women's? But I'd be ashamed.

DIONYSOS You're not so eager to watch maenads, any more?

PENTHEUS What dress do you intend to clothe me in?

DIONYSOS First, on your head, I'll make your hair much longer.

PENTHEUS And the next piece of my adornment—what will it be?

DIONYSOS Full-length robes that reach your feet, and a headband.   950

PENTHEUS Is there anything more you'll add to this?

DIONYSOS Yes—a thyrsos in your hand, and a spotted fawn skin.

PENTHEUS No—I wouldn't wear a woman's clothes.

DIONYSOS To war against the Bakkhai means great bloodshed.

PENTHEUS You're right. First I must go and spy on them.

DIONYSOS That's wiser than to hunt down evils with evil.

PENTHEUS But how can I go through the town and not be seen?

DIONYSOS Along deserted streets—I'll show you where.

PENTHEUS Anything's better than the Bakkhai laughing that they've
          won.

DIONYSOS So we'll go in [. . .]

PENTHEUS   [. . .] I have to ponder what to do.   960

DIONYSOS Of course! Whatever you decide, my plan is set.

PENTHEUS I think that I'll go in. For I must either
          Proceed against them armed, or suffer your advice.

He goes into the royal house.

DIONYSOS

Returning to address the chorus:

          Women! The man is heading toward our net.
          He will come to the Bakkhai, where he'll meet
          His justice—death. And now, Dionysos, things
          Will turn your way—for you are not far off.
          Let's take our vengeance on him: first, derange
          His mind and put him in a giddy frenzy—
          For in his right mind he will never want   970
          To wear a woman's clothes, but if he drives
          His chariot off the road of sanity,
          He'll wear them. Then, I want him to be laughed at
          By everyone when he is led through town
          A man-turned-woman—after his terrible threats!
          I'll go dress Pentheus in what he'll wear
          To Hades—sacrificed by his mother's hand.
          And he will know that Dionysos, son
          Of Zeus, was born a god in full, and is
          Most terrible to mortals and most gentle.   980

He follows PENTHEUS *into the royal house.*

The CHORUS *dance and sing.*

CHORUS   *Third stasimon (fourth ode)*
    Will I ever celebrate   *strophe*
    All night with white foot
    Flashing in the Bakkhic dance?
    Will I ever fling back
    My head and let the air
    Of heaven touch my throat
    With dew, like a fawn at play
    In the green joy of meadows?—
        Having escaped just when the frightening
        Hunt encircled it, when the guards were standing
           watch   990
    Close around and it has
    Leapt the strongly woven
    Nets and then the hunter
    Has cried the hounds
    Onward and the fawn with utmost
    Straining effort has run
    Fast as storm-wind and raced
        Through river-watered plains
    To reach the deserted wilds and take joy
    In being where no mortals come and the leafy   1000
    Forest stands above thick shade?

    What is wise? What gift from the gods
    Do mortals judge more beautiful
    Than to hold our outstretched
    Strong hand over an enemy's head?
    What is beautiful is what is always loved.

    The unremitting power   *antistrophe*
    Of the divine begins only
    Slowly to move, but
    Always moves. It brings   1010
    To reckoning those mortals
    Who honor senseless
    Arrogance and who with mad
    Beliefs do not give
        The gods their due. For in their intricate way

       The gods conceal the slow foot of time
To lull us while they hunt down
The desecrator. Never
Should one think or act
As if above what is   1020
Accepted as the law
Of things. It costs so little
To believe that it does rule—
       Whatever the divine may be,
Whatever over long ages of time
Is accepted as lawful, always,
And comes to be through nature.

What is wise? What gift from the gods
Do mortals judge more beautiful
Than to hold our outstretched   1030
Strong hand over an enemy's head?
What is beautiful is what is always loved.

Happy is he who escapes   *epode*
A storm at sea and finds safe harbor.
Happy is he who has risen above
Great toils. In different ways,
Some persons outdo others
In their wealth and power.
       And hopes are as many as those who hope—
       Some will end in rich reward, others in nothing.   1040
But those whose lives are happy
Day by day—those
I call the blessèd.

SCENE IV

DIONYSOS *enters from the royal house; he calls back inside.*

DIONYSOS You, Pentheus!—rushing toward what you should
              Not rush to see, zealous for what should not
              Evoke such zeal—you, Pentheus, come out!
              Come out in front of the house, reveal yourself
              To me, come out here wearing women's clothes,

77

Clothes of maenads, clothes of Bakkhai, ready
To spy on your own mother and her troupe.   1050

> PENTHEUS *enters from the royal house, dressed as a woman,*
> *wearing a wig, a sash around his head, and a long linen*
> *robe like a dress, and carrying a thyrsos.*

You have the very form of Kadmos' daughters.

PENTHEUS In fact, it seems to me I see two suns,
A double seven-gated fortress of Thebes.
You lead me forward, so it seems, as a bull,
You seem to have grown two horns upon your head.
Were you, all this time, an animal?
For you have certainly been . . . bullified.

DIONYSOS The god who earlier was ill-disposed toward us, comes
with us,
At peace with us. You're seeing what you should see,
now.

PENTHEUS How do I appear? Don't you think I'm standing   1060
The way that Ino stands? Or as Agauë — Mother — does?

DIONYSOS Looking at you, I seem to see them, here.
But a lock of hair has fallen out of place,
It's not where I tucked it up beneath your sash.

PENTHEUS Inside, when I was shaking it back and forth,
Acting like the Bakkhai, it came loose.

DIONYSOS But since our task is to take good care of you,
I'll put it back — but hold your head up straight.

PENTHEUS Arrange it all! I'm dedicated to you.

DIONYSOS Your belt is slack. And then the pleats of your robe   1070
Do not hang straight, below your ankles, either.

PENTHEUS No, it seems to me they don't, on my right side.
But on this side it's all straight at my heel.

78

DIONYSOS   You'll certainly think I'm the first of all your friends,
           When you're surprised to see how modest the Bakkhai
               are.

PENTHEUS   Which way is more as the Bakkhai do — to hold
           The thyrsos in my right hand or my left?

DIONYSOS   Raise it right-handed, in time with your right foot.
           I commend you on how changed your mind is.

PENTHEUS   Would I be able to carry Mount Kitháiron,   1080
           Canyons and Bakkhai, too, on my own shoulders?

DIONYSOS   Yes, if you wished. Before, your mind was sick,
           But now you have the kind of mind you should have.

PENTHEUS   Should we bring strong bars? Or should I use bare hands
               to pry it up,
           And set my arm or shoulder underneath the mountain
               top?

DIONYSOS   Don't go destroying the shrines of nymphs up there,
           And the haunts of Pan, where he plays his reed pipes.

PENTHEUS   You're right. It's not by force that we must conquer
           The women. I will hide among the trees.

DIONYSOS   You will be hidden as you should be hidden —   1090
           A stealthy man who goes to spy on the maenads.

PENTHEUS   I think they're flitting through the woods like birds,
           Then fluttering in the nets of making love.

DIONYSOS   And isn't that just what you'll guard against?
           You will catch them, if you are not caught first.

PENTHEUS   Escort me up the widest street in Thebes,
           Since I'm the only man who'd dare to do this.

DIONYSOS   You alone must bear all this for Thebes —
           Just you! That's why the contest you deserve

79

Awaits you. Follow me—I'll escort you   1100
To salvation. But someone else will bring you back . . .

PENTHEUS   . . . She who gave birth to me.

DIONYSOS You'll be remarkable to everyone . . .

PENTHEUS   That's why I'm going.

DIONYSOS You will be carried home . . .

PENTHEUS   . . . It's soft delight you speak of!

DIONYSOS . . . in your mother's arms.

PENTHEUS   You'll force me to be spoiled.

DIONYSOS Yes, true spoiling.

PENTHEUS   But I only claim my due.

                                                    PENTHEUS *exits.*

DIONYSOS

                              His words follow PENTHEUS *off stage:*

        Terror, terror and awe surround you, now.
        You'll suffer something terrible, you'll find
        A fame that rises all the way to heaven.
        Open your arms, Agauë and your sisters,
        Daughter-seed of Kadmos—I bring this youth   1110
        To the great contest, and both Bromios
        And I will win. What happens next will show.

                                            He exits.

The CHORUS *dance and sing*

CHORUS   *Fourth stasimon (fifth ode)*

Hounds of Fury, rush to the mountain,   *strophe*
Where the daughters of Kadmos gather their troupe.
     Sting them to madness
Against this man who mimics woman,
The madman spying on the maenads!
His mother from some tall pole or rocky cliff
Will catch first sight of him,
She'll call out to the maenads,   1120
     "Who is this, O Bakkhai,
Who has come, who has come to the mountain,
To the mountain, searching for us, O daughters of
        Kadmos,
We who run freely over the mountainside?
What was it that gave birth to him? He was not born
       From the blood of women, but from a lionness,
Or he's descended from the Libyan Gorgons!

Let Justice appear! Let her
Carry a sword for killing,
     And stab through the throat   1130
Ekhíon's unjust, ungodly, unlawful
Earthborn offspring!

Because he, of lawless attitudes   *antistrophe*
And sacrilegious rage against your mystic rites,
     Bakkhos, and those of your mother,
Sets out with maddened heart and false ideals
To conquer by force what is unconquerable!
Him, death will not be slow to teach to have
Right thoughts about the gods.
Whereas to live rightly as a mortal is to live without the
       penalty of grief.   1140
     Let the clever be clever,
But I rejoice in hunting
What is great and is clear, what leads
Life to right things, what leads us
By day and by night to be holy

        And reverent, to cast aside all customs
    That do not belong to justice, and to honor the gods.

        Let Justice appear! Let her
    Carry a sword for killing,
            And stab through the throat   1150
    Ekhíon's unjust, ungodly, unlawful
    Earthborn offspring!

        Appear as a bull! As a snake   *epode*
    With many heads, for us to see you!
    As a lion with a mane of fire!
    Go, great Bakkhos, O beast!, with your laughing face
    Circle in a net of death this hunter of Bakkhai
    Who falls now under the trampling herd
            Of the maenads!

                        SCENE V

        As if many hours had passed, a new MESSENGER *enters.*

SECOND MESSENGER O house once fortunate in all of Greece!   1160
            House of that patriarch of Sidon who planted
            In the soil the dragon-crop that was born from earth
            As men—how I must grieve over you, now,
            Although I am your slave—but even so!

    CHORUS What is it? Do you bring some news of the Bakkhai?

SECOND MESSENGER Pentheus, Ekhíon's child, is dead.

        CHORUS   *Singing.*

        O Lord Bromios, revealed as a great god!

SECOND MESSENGER What do you mean? What did you say? Do you
                Rejoice at what my master suffered, woman?

        CHORUS   *Singing.*

    82

I am a stranger here. I sing a foreign song to cry in joy.   1170
No longer do I cower in fear of being chained.

SECOND MESSENGER Do you consider Thebes as so unmanly
     That you will not be punished for what you say?

    CHORUS   *Singing.*

    Dionysos, Dionysos, not Thebes,
    Has the power to rule me!

SECOND MESSENGER You women can be pardoned for that, but joy
     At suffering others have already borne is wrong.

    CHORUS   *Singing.*

    Tell it to me, describe it to me, how does
    The unjust man, the agent of injustice, die?

SECOND MESSENGER After we left the settled ground of Thebes,   1180
     And crossed the streams of Asópos, we climbed up
     Steep slopes of Mount Kitháiron—Pentheus
     And I, for I was close behind my master
     And that Stranger who escorted us on our
     Procession to the place where we would watch.
     We were careful not to speak, nor to make
     A sound when stepping, when we hid ourselves
     In the grassy valley so that we could see them
     Without them seeing us. There was a ravine
     Surrounded by high cliffs, braided by streams,   1190
     And shaded by stands of pine, and there the maenads
     Were sitting, their hands engaged in pleasant tasks—
     Some put new ivy curls at the crown of a staff,
     And others—like young fillies that had been
     Unharnesssed from embroidered yokes—at rest,
     Called out a Bakkhic song to one another.
      Pentheus—poor, reckless man—who was
     Unable to view the women, said, "O Stranger,
     From where we stand I cannot see to where
     Those faking maenads are, but if I climbed   1200

A tall-necked tree, on higher ground, I'd see
Clearly what those shameless maenads are doing."
          And then the Stranger performed some wondrous
               deeds—
He reached to the top branch of a fir tree
As tall as the sky and pulled it downward, down,
Down till it touched the black earth and it formed
Half a circle, like a bow drawn back
Or the wheel-curve that's traced by the taut end
Of a pegged string. That is, with his bare hands
The Stranger bent the mountain fir in a way   1210
No mortal could. And seating Pentheus
Among the branches, he began to let
The tree straighten itself, passing it through
His hands so gently that it didn't buck
And throw its rider off, till it rose as far
As the air of heaven, my master on its back,
At the top. Instead of seeing maenads, though,
He was seen by them—for, as soon as he rose
Up there, the Stranger disappeared, and a voice
From heaven—Dionysos' voice, I'd think—   1220
Cried out, "Young women! I have brought you the man
Who makes a mockery of you and me
And of my mystic rites! Now take revenge
On him!" And as the voice proclaimed these things,
A rising light of holy fire was set
Between the earth and heaven. The high air
Was still; the leaves of all the trees were still—
You would not have heard one animal
Stir or cry out.
                    The women, since the sound
Had reached their ears from no apparent source,   1230
Stood up and looked this way and that. Again
Came the command, and when they recognized
That it was Dionysos' voice, these women,
Daughters of Kadmos—[Agauë and all her kindred
Of the same seed,] and all the Bakkhai—rushed
At him as fast as doves, [but by the quickness
Of their running feet]. And mad with the god's breath
They leapt the icy torrents and jagged boulders.
          When they saw my master sitting atop

That tall fir tree, at first they picked up stones   1240
And flung them at him with tremendous strength,
They clambered up on rocks as high as towers,
Some threw fir branches like crude javelins,
And others hurled their thyrsoi through the air
Of heaven at poor wretched Pentheus.
But not a thing could reach him. And as his height
Was greater than their fury, there he sat,
Caught in an impossible place. But at last
They started tearing up the roots of the tree,
Striking with oak branches like thunderbolts—   1250
With bars of wood, not iron, they used as levers.
When all this toil proved useless, Agauë said,
"Maenads! Make a circle and take hold
Of the trunk—let's capture this tree-climbing beast
And stop him from revealing to anyone
The secret dances of the god." They put
Countless hands on the tree and pulled it out
Of the earth. Sitting high up, high he is
When he starts to fall, and hurtling toward the ground
With countless groaning cries, he crashes down.   1260
Pentheus knew that now he was at the edge
Of calamity. And his mother was the first,
As priestess, to begin the slaughter. She
Falls on him and he tears the headband from
His hair so that wretched Agauë will
Recognize him, not kill him, and he touches
Her cheek as he begins to say to her,
"Mother, it's Pentheus, your child! It's me!
You gave birth to me in Ekhíon's house.
Have pity on me, Mother! Don't kill me   1270
For my wrongdoing!" But she was slavering,
Her eyes rolled up, she was possessed by Bakkhos,
Not thinking as she should, and Pentheus
Did not persuade her. Taking with both her hands
His left forearm and setting her foot hard
Against the ribs of this ill-fated man,
She tore his shoulder out—not by her strength
But by the ease the god gave to her hands.
And Ino had destroyed his other side,
Breaking up his flesh, and Autonoë   1280

And the Bakkhai mobbed him and everyone was
    screaming
At the same time—he groaning his last breath,
And they raising the war cry of their triumph.
    One of them was flaunting a severed arm,
Another held a foot still shod for hunting,
His ribs were being bared by clawing nails,
And all with bloodied hands were playing games
By tossing hunks of the flesh of Pentheus.
His corpse lies scattered among the rugged rocks
And deep within the forest in thick foliage—   1290
It will be difficult to find it all
Again.
       His pitiful head, which his mother took
In her own hands, she put at the top of a thyrsos,
She carries it across Kitháiron's slope
As if it were a lion's head, she leaves
Her sisters with the dancing troupe of maenads.
Rejoicing in this hunt that is so un-
Lucky, she comes to town calling to Bakkhos,
Her fellow hunter, her comrade in the chase—
Triumphant Dionysos, through whose power   1300
What she wins for a trophy is her tears.
    I must go now, away from this disaster,
Before Agaüe comes back to the house.
Wise moderation and a reverence
For what is of the gods—this is what's best.
And this, I think, of all possessions owned
By mortals, is the wisest one to use.

He exits.

The CHORUS *dance and sing*

CHORUS   *Fifth stasimon (sixth ode)*
    Let us dance the Bakkhic dance!
    Let us shout the doom
Of Pentheus, descended from a dragon-snake!   1310
    He put on women's clothes,

He carried the fennel-rod of Hades,
The thyrsos that is the warrant of his death!
And at his fall, a bull was in command!
    You Bakkhai of the house of Kadmos,
You have changed your famous hymn of triumph
    To tears, to lamentation.
Beautiful contest — to plunge her hand in the blood
    Of her child, to drip with it!

I see Agauë, mother of Pentheus, .   1320
With rolling eyes she's rushing toward the house.
Welcome her to the revelers of the god of rapture!

CLOSING SCENE

AGAUË *enters carrying a mask before her as if it were a*
head; alone, she dances as she sings, along with the
CHORUS, *this ode:*

AGAUË You Lydian Bakkhai . . .   *strophe*

CHORUS   O, why do you call to me, woman?

AGAUË Because, from the mountain,
    And for this house, we bring in a blessèd hunt,
    A fresh-cut tendril.

CHORUS I see you, I welcome you as our sister-reveler.

AGAUË Without nets, I captured
    This young creature,
    As you see.   1330

CHORUS In what part of the wilderness?

AGAUË   Mount Kitháiron . . .

CHORUS Mount Kitháiron?

AGAUË   . . . killed him.

87

CHORUS Who struck him first?

AGAUË   That honor was mine.
        Blessed Agauë I am called, in the sacred troupes.

CHORUS Who else?

AGAUË   It was Kadmos — his . . .

CHORUS Kadmos' what?

AGAUË   His daughters —
        But after me, after me — who put their hands on this wild
                creature.
        Most fortunate was the hunt.

        So share this feast.   *antistrophe*

CHORUS   What, poor woman? — share this?

AGAUË This young bull-calf   1340
        Had just begun to sprout a little beard
        To match his delicate crest of hair, like a helmet.

CHORUS Yes, his hair makes him seem a beast of the wild.

AGAUË Bakkhos the wise
        Hunter cunningly set the maenads
        On this beast.

CHORUS For the Lord is a hunter.

AGAUË Are you praising him?

CHORUS   We are praising.

AGAUË And soon the rest of Kadmos' family . . .

CHORUS And Pentheus, your son, among them . . .

AGAUË   . . . will praise his mother —   1350
        For having caught this prey so like a lion.

CHORUS Strange prey.

AGAUË   Killed in a strange way.

CHORUS Are you exulting in this?

AGAUË   I rejoice
        In what great things this hunt achieved,
        Great things revealed to all!

                                        End of ode and dance.

CHORUS Then show the townspeople the prey, poor woman,
        That brought you victory, that you bring with you.

AGAUË Thebans! You who live in this citadel
        Of lovely towers, come see the beast, the prey
        We daughters of Kadmos hunted down—and not   1360
        With nets nor spear-throwers but with the points
        Of our own white-fingered hands. What need is there
        For hurling useless lances? Why be proud
        Of what spear-crafters make? We caught this one
        With just our hands and tore the beast apart!
        Where's my old father, now? Let him come here.
        Where's Pentheus, my child? Let him bring tall
        Well-built ladders to raise against the house,
        Let him fix to the high triglyphs this head
        Of a lion which I myself have hunted down.   1370

                KADMOS enters, *followed by* ATTENDANTS *carrying a*
                litter on which the parts of PENTHEUS' *body lie.*

KADMOS Follow me as you carry the sad weight
        Of Pentheus—follow me, men, to the front
        Of the house. I bring his body with me after
        I toiled in endless searching till I found it
        Lying in the rough canyons of Mount Kithairon,
        The pieces scattered here and there in thick
        Impenetrable woods. For when I had
        Already come back to the town with old
        Teiresias, from the Bakkhai, and had passed

89

Within these walls, again, I heard from someone   1380
Of what outrageous acts my daughters had
Committed. And once more to the mountainside
I went, and retrieved the child who died at the hands
Of the maenads. And I saw Autonoë,
Who bore Aktáion, son of Aristáios;
And Ino, too, there, in the thickets, both
Of them still stung to frenzies, wretched women.
But someone said Agauë was dancing down
With Bakkhic steps toward home.

                                      He turns to AGAUË.

                          Nor was that
Untrue, for I see her—unhappy sight.   1390

AGAUË Father! Now you may boast that of all mortals
       You begot by far the best of daughters—
       All of us, but me especially,
       Who left the loom and shuttles for greater things—
       The hunting of wild beasts with my bare hands.
       See what I carry in my arms—the reward
       I've won, the prize for prowess, which will hang high
       On your house: take it, Father, in your hands,
       Exult in my good hunt and call your friends
       To feast, for you are blessèd, blessèd, now,   1400
       By what we have already brought to be.

KADMOS

                                                   Aside.

O grief too great to be grasped, grief . . . Murder
Done already by such pitiable hands.

                                                To AGAUË.

Yes, what a perfect sacrificial victim
You have struck down, for the gods, to welcome Thebes
And me to such a feast. What suffering!—
First yours, then mine. The god, lord Bromios,
Destroys us justly, yes—but goes too far,

For one who was born into this very house.

AGAUË Old age in humankind is so ill-tempered,   1410
And has such scowling eyes! I wish my child
Were good at hunting, and were made just like
His mother, when with the young men of Thebes
He would go pursuing wild beasts—but instead,
The only thing that he can do is fight
Against divinity. You must rebuke him,
Father! Would someone call him into my sight,
To see his mother, me, most happily blessed?

KADMOS

Groaning.

Oh. . . . When you begin to understand
What you have done, you'll suffer terribly.   1420
But if, till the end, you were to stay like this,
As you are now, you'd not be fortunate,
Although in your trance you're not unfortunate.

AGAUË But what is painful, or not good, in this?

KADMOS First, look up just a moment at the sky.

AGAUË All right. Why do you say for me to look there?

KADMOS Is it the same, or did it seem to change?

AGAUË It's brighter than before, and seems more clear.

KADMOS And is there still a fluttering in your spirit?

AGAUË I don't know what you mean. But somehow, I do   1430
Feel more myself, my mind is different.

KADMOS Will you listen to me, and answer me?

AGAUË Yes, Father—I've forgotten what we said.

KADMOS To what house did you go when you were married?

AGAUË You gave me to Ekhíon—"the Planted Man," as they say.

KADMOS And in his house, what child did you bear for your
husband?

AGAUË Pentheus—from my union with his father.

KADMOS Now, then—whose countenance do you have in your
arms?

AGAUË

Not looking, yet.

A lion's—so the women said, in the hunt.

KADMOS Look at it now—it's not much toil to look.   1440

AGAUË Oh! What am I seeing? What's this I'm holding in my
hands?

KADMOS Look closely now, and understand it better.

AGAUË Doomed woman that I am, I see the greatest grief.

KADMOS Does it still appear to you to be a lion?

AGAUË No. I am doomed. It's Pentheus' head I'm holding.

KADMOS Yes—something that was mourned before you recognized
it.

AGAUË Who killed him? How did this get in my hands?

KADMOS Unhappy truth, how wrong the moment when you come
to us!

AGAUË Speak! My heart is leaping in fear of what's to come.

KADMOS You and your sisters were the ones who killed him.   1450

AGAUË Where did he die? At home? Where did this happen?

92

KADMOS Just where the hounds once tore apart Aktáion.

AGAUË But why did this man, destined for ill, climb Mount
                    Kitháiron?

KADMOS To mock the god, and all your Bakkhic revels.

AGAUË But how did we ourselves get to the mountain?

KADMOS You all went mad, and all the town was driven to Bakkhic
                    frenzy.

AGAUË Now I see that Dionysos crushed us.

KADMOS Yes, outraged by outrage. For none of you acknowledged
                    him as a god.

AGAUË Father—where's the dear body of my child?

KADMOS I made a long hard search for it; I bring it with me.   1460

AGAUË Has all of it—the limbs—been placed together decently?

KADMOS [No, not completely, for you still hold his head.]

                              She approaches the body of PENTHEUS.

[AGAUË Pity me—for I who once was blessed
                    With happiness, am wretched now. These men
                    Will not put you properly in your tomb.
                    But then, how can I? And in what sort
                    Of tomb? And covered with what sort of robes?
                    How can I lift these limbs, and kiss torn flesh
                    That I myself gave birth to? How can I,
                    As miserable as I am, take care of you   1470
                    And lift you to my breast? What wailing dirge
                    Can I sing?
                                        We must bury him, but what
                    Small consolation this is to the dead!
                    Come then, old man, and let us fit the head
                    Of this poor child into its proper place,
                    And fit together all his body as best

We can, the parts in harmony again.
O face most dear to me, and cheeks of a child!

> *She lays the head in place, then arranges the bloody re-*
> *mains, piece by piece, as she speaks. Finally, with robes*
> *brought by* KADMOS' ATTENDANTS *from the royal*
> *house, she covers the body.*

Look—with this veil, I cover up your face.
With these fresh robes I shelter you, your blood-   1480
Smeared limbs, gashed and sundered from each other.]
[. . .]

To KADMOS:

How much of my madness did Pentheus share with me?

KADMOS He proved himself to be like you—he refused
To revere the gods. Uniting everyone
In one great ruin—all of you and himself—
He destroyed this house—including me, for I,
Who have no sons, see this one child of yours,
Poor woman, die the worst, most shameful death.
Through him this house began to see, once more.

He addresses the body.

O child, born to my daughter, scourge of the city,   1490
You held our house together. No one dared
Insult this old man, if they saw that you
Were near, for you'd inflict just punishment.
But now I'll be cast out of my house, dishonored—
The great Kadmos, who planted the Theban race,
And reaped the fairest crop. You most-loved man
(For even though you exist no more, still you
Remain for me the dearest of all, child)—
No longer will you touch your hand to my chin,
Nor put your arms around me, nor will you call me   1500
Your mother's father, nor say, "Has someone been
Unjust to you, old Sir? Dishonored you?
Who disturbs your heart by troubling you?

Tell me — I'll punish him who's unjust to you,
Father." But today I'm torn by sorrow,
And you are ruined, your mother to be pitied,
Your whole clan ruined. Anyone who feels
Superior to the gods should study this:
Pentheus is dead — believe in the gods!

CHORUS Kadmos, I grieve for you, but your grandchild received   1510
the justice he deserved, although for you it is hard.

AGAUË Father! You see how my life is overturned. [. . .]

DIONYSOS *appears on the roof of the royal house.*

[DIONYSOS . . .

Agauë, you must leave this city, now,
That was so eager for killing. You must know
And live the punishment that you deserve.
I shall proclaim the sufferings that this man,
Kadmos, will bear: against me you have brought
Unseemly words, false claims that from a man,
A mortal, Sémelê gave birth to me.
Nor was this affront sufficient outrage   1520
For you — therefore was Pentheus killed by those
From whom he least deserved it, because he used
Chains and taunting words against me: this
Was what your people did, in frenzied rage,
Against the benefactor who had loved them.
Pentheus deserved his suffering.
The evils you and all your people must
Now suffer, I will not conceal from you:
You shall leave this city as a captive
Of barbarians, a slave, in exile from   1530
Your home. For it is prophesied that you
Must make your way through every foreign land,
A prisoner held at spear-point — you will endure
Innumerable woes. Because you all
Must pay the penalty for the foul pollution
Of unholy killing, you shall leave this city
And look upon your native land no longer.
It is not holy for murderers to stay

Among the tombs of those whom they have killed.
Man of misfortune, to city after city   1540
You will go, bearing the yoke of slavery.

KADMOS From all that you have done, it is clear to me you are a
            god.]

DIONYSOS And then, you will be changed to a dragon-snake,
            Your wife, made monstrous, too, will take the shape
            Of a serpent: Harmonía, Ares' daughter,
            Whom you took to wife, even though you
            Were mortal. And you and she, as was foretold
            By an oracle of Zeus, will drive an oxcart
            For a chariot, and lead barbarians
            And ravage many cities with numberless troops.   1550
            But after they despoil the oracle
            Of Apollo, they will undergo a journey
            Homeward of misery. And yet the god
            Ares will save both you and Harmonía
            And give you new life in the land of the blessèd.
            I, Dionysos, say these things as the child
            Not of a mortal father but of Zeus.
            If you had chosen to think rightly when
            You did not wish to, you'd be happy, now,
            Having gained as your ally the child of Zeus.   1560

KADMOS We beg you, Dionysos—we have been unjust to you.

DIONYSOS You understood too late; when you should have known
            us, you did not.

KADMOS Now we see, but you are too hard on us.

DIONYSOS Yes. Because I, born a god, was so dishonored by you.

KADMOS It is not fitting for gods to rage as if they were the same as
            mortals.

DIONYSOS Long ago, my father Zeus ordained all this.

AGAUË Aiee. It is decided, Father. Exile, misery.

96

DIONYSOS Why, then, do you delay what you must do?

KADMOS To what an overwhelming end we've come,
         My child—you and your poor wretched sisters,   1570
         And I, also. I must go out among
         Barbarians—an old uprooted settler.
         And more than that, the gods ordain that I
         Myself will lead a horde back into Greece,
         A rabble army of barbarians!
         Harmonía—Ares' daughter!—a snake!
         And I, a serpent, too. Attacking Greek
         Altars and tombs, commanding many spearmen.
         Nor, in my wretchedness, will I be freed
         From suffering: not even after I sail   1580
         The River Acheron, that plummets so
         Steeply downward, will I be given peace.

AGAUË O Father, I am exiled deprived of you!

KADMOS Why, my miserable child, do you embrace me,
         Since I am like a useless old white swan?

AGAUË But where can I go now, cast out of my fatherland?

KADMOS I do not know. Your father is a weak ally.

AGAUË Good bye, my house. Good bye,
         City of my father's kin.
         I leave in sorrow, banned   1590
         From my own bedroom.

KADMOS Go, now, my child, to Aristáios' house . . .

AGAUË Father, I grieve for you . . .

KADMOS   And I for you, my child.
         And I am weeping for your sisters.

AGAUË It is a terrible blow
         That Lord Dionysos
         Has sent down on your house.

KADMOS   Yes, because of us he suffered things
          So terrible, dishonored was his name in Thebes.

AGAUË   Farewell, Father.

KADMOS   Farewell, my forlorn daughter—   1600
          Although you cannot now fare well.

AGAUË

                                            To the CHORUS.

              Lead me, companion escorts, where
              With my sad sisters we'll be exiled.
              Let me go where neither polluted
              Mount Kitháiron can see me,
              Nor can I see Mount Kitháiron,
              Where no reminding thyrsos has been dedicated.
              Let such things be for other Bakkhai.

                    AGAUË *and* KADMOS *exit in opposite directions.*

CHORUS   *Singing as they exit.*

              Many are the shapes of what's divine,
              Many unforeseen events the gods design.   1610
              What seemed most likely was not fulfilled;
              What was unlikely, the god has willed.
              Such were the things that end in this decline.

NOTES ON THE TEXT

BIBLIOGRAPHICAL NOTE

The commentary of E. R. Dodds (Introduction, note 24) remains fundamental for all serious study of the play. Useful comments are also to be found in Esposito (Introduction, note 4); Ieranò (Introduction, note 35); G. S. Kirk, ed. and trans., *The Bakkhai by Euripides* (Englewood Cliffs, N.J., 1982); Jeanne Roux, *Les Bacchantes d'Euripide* (Paris, 1970–72), 2 vols.; Seaford, *Euripides, Bacchae* (1996, n. 4, p. 5); R. P. Winnington-Ingram, *Euripides and Dionysus* (Cambridge, 1948). The most authoritative recent critical edition of the Greek text is James Diggle, *Euripidis Fabulae*, III, Oxford Classical Texts (Oxford, 1994). These works are cited by author's name below. Detailed bibliographies may be found in Ieranò, Seaford, and the second edition of C. Segal, *Dionysiac Poetics and Euripides' Bacchae*, (1997, n. 4, p. 5).

1–73 *prologue* Euripides usually begins his plays with a long speech by a major character, occasionally a god, and this figure sets out the background and future course of events. When a god or other supernatural figure speaks the prologue (as in *Alcestis, Hippolytos, Hecuba, Trojan Women,* and *Ion*) and a different god appears at the end, that divinity in the prologue exits and remains aloof from the rest of the action. Here Dionysos, in the guise of the Lydian Stranger, will continue on the stage as a major participant in the events and then reappear as deus ex machine at the end. His announcement signals the central role of disguise and recognition in the play and is also consistent with the importance of epiphanies, wearing masks, and changing shapes in the cults and myths of Dionysos.

1–2 *son of Zeus . . . Dionysos* Dionysos is often etymologized as son of Zeus (*Dios huios*). Other etymologies include a link with Dionysos' sacred mountain, Nysa.

2–3 *Semelé, Kadmos' daughter, gave a fiery birth* Refers to the birth of Dionysos from Semelé's incinerated body after her destruction (engineered by Hera) by Zeus' lightning. Zeus then rescues the infant Dionysos from her womb and preserves him in his thigh, a tale to which the play several times alludes. See below on 11–12.

11–12 *the immortal rage / And violence of Hera against my mother* Hera's wrathful persecution of the children born from Zeus' loves is a recurrent feature of Greek myth. A papyrus fragment of Aeschylus' lost tragedy, *Semelé or the Water Carriers*, confirms that Hera came to Thebes disguised as a priestess in order to trick Semelé into her fatal request from Zeus; see H. W. Smyth, ed. and trans., *Aeschylus*, Loeb Classical Library, vol. 2, ed. Hugh Lloyd-Jones (Cambridge, Mass., 1971), 566–71; see also Plato, *Republic* 2.381d.

17–23 *Leaving the country of the Phrygians, / And the Lydians . . . Asia Minor* The Greeks often trace Dionysos' origins to Asia Minor (and also to Thrace, northeast of Greece). On Phrygia see below on 78–79. Whereas in their myths the Greeks depict Dionysos as a late, foreign import, the appearance of his name on Mycenaean Linear B tablets shows that he was probably established in Greece by at least the thirteenth century B.C.E.; see Introduction, p. 8.

21–22 *Baktrians . . . Medes . . . Arabia* The first two places belong to central Asia, and all three lie at the remote fringes of Greek geographical knowledge at this period. It has sometimes been suspected that these lines are a later interpolation, reflecting a world subsequent to the conquests of Alexander the Great in the late fourth century B.C.E. But Euripides' references imply no very specific knowledge, and the Greeks were familiar with the Persian Empire from the late sixth century. The far-flung geography suggests both the universalism of the god and his exotic appearance to the inhabitants of the first Greek city he visits.

30 *It was Thebes* Thebes, the birthplace of Dionysos, was famous for its worship of the god; logically, then, it is the first Greek city to receive his worship.

32–33 *fawn skin . . . thyrsos . . . ivy* These familiar trappings of Dionysiac worship are frequently depicted on numerous vases from the sixth century B.C.E. on. His female worshipers on these vases often wear fawn skins and brandish the thyrsos, a long fennel stalk (also called the narthex) tipped at the end with a bunch of ivy leaves. Its potential use as a weapon (here *javelin*), as it sometimes is on fifth-century vases, foreshadows the dangerous side of maenadic ecstasy later in the play (see line 874). But the maenads also use the thyrsos to call forth water, milk, and wine from the earth (lines 811–17), and in that scene it also drips with honey.

45–50 *To a frenzy, out of their very homes . . . driven from their homes . . . madness* From the outset, the play presents two groups of Dionysos' female worshipers, the Lydian women of the chorus and the women of Thebes. The Lydian women are his willing devotees, are in the city with their god, and (with one exception) are never called maenads or mad. The women of Thebes are devotees by constraint. Dionysos has driven them to Mt. Kithairon outside Thebes, and they are maenads in the literal sense, that is, *mad women.* Dionysiac cult allows women to indulge in the open expression of violent emotions that fifth-century Athens (like the mythical Theban king Pentheus) regarded with suspicion. The approved behavior of women in this society is summed up by the term *sôphrosynê* (modesty, self-control, sound good sense) and it also implies submission to male authority. It is a key concept in the play, claimed by both sides. In his accusations of the maenads, Pentheus consistently uses it in the authoritarian sense — as the opposite of license, disorder, and disobedience — whereas the chorus and the Lydian Stranger claim for Dionysos' worshipers a kind of *sôphrosynê* that Pentheus cannot understand, using the word in its more general sense of good mental health, a sound and balanced mind.

52–53 *They sit on rocks . . . pale green pines* In contrast to most of the Olympian gods, Dionysos' shrines are often (though not exclusively) in the country; and his worship, as here described, may also take place outside the city.

58–59 *Kadmos has handed all authority . . .* The play offers no explanation for the absence of Ekhion, one of the Planted Men and Pentheus' father, who would be the logical successor to Kadmos.

60 *at war with deity itself* Euripides' verb, *theomakhein,* (literally, to fight against the god) occurs several times later in the play (383–84, 638, 738–39, 1415–16) and casts Pentheus into the role of the god's monstrous antagonist in the resistance myth that characterizes the acceptance of Dionysos' cult in Greece. See 630–38, with the note on this passage below. The story of the Thracian king Lykourgos is a similar myth of a king who disastrously *fights against the god.* See Introduction, p. 15.

68–69 *Theban city / Angrily takes up weapons* This full-scale battle between maenads and the forces of the city never actually takes place and so is sometimes regarded as a narrative trick, a suggestion of an event that will not in fact occur in the play. Yet Pentheus does threaten such a battle (896–902), and it is realized in miniature in the First Messenger's speech when the maenads defeat the herdsmen and attack the villages on Kithairon (858–77). The lines also foreshadow the dangerous side of the Theban maenads, who prove capable of fighting as if in military formation (see 830–41).

78–79 *the Phyrgian drums / Invented by Mother Rhea and by me* The chorus here draws on a common identification between the Greek goddess, Rhea, mother of Zeus and Hera, and the Phrygian mother goddess of mountains and ecstatic rites, Kybelé, who is named explicitly later, line 104.

84–202 *parode* or *parodos* The first entrance of the chorus into the orchestra, always a spectacular moment in the Greek theater. The chorus wear elaborate costumes and here are accompanied by the *aulos* (closer to an oboe than a flute), and probably by the drums (actually more like tambourines) to which the chorus allude in lines 154–65. The dominant meter of this ode is the ionic a minore, $\cup \cup - -$, which recurs in several other odes as a rhythmical leitmotif that helps unify the play.

87 *no toil nor weariness* The peace that Dionysos brings to those who accept him is a recurrent feature of the play. It is shown in the initial behavior of the maenads in both the Messengers' speeches and in the contrast between Pentheus' frenzy and the Stranger's cool detachment in the scene in the stables (lines 719–20, 736–38). See below on lines 720 and 744–45.

99–100 *who joins his spirit / With the holy worshipers* this extraordinary phrase expresses the fusion of the individual worshiper with the collective emotions of the whole band of worshipers. The Greek, *thiaseuetai psukhan,* is, literally, something like "makes himself or herself part of the holy band [*thiasos*] with his/her inner spirit or personal consciousness" [*psukhan*].

128 *the god with the horns of a bull* Dionysos' identification with the bull (symbol of fertility, energy, animal exuberance) recurs throughout the play (e.g. 717–19, 1054–56, 1153, 1314). His epithets in cult and in poetry often allude to his taurine form, and in the Hellenistic period, he is often represented with the horns of a bull. Within the *Bakkhai* Dionysos

appears as a bull and also receives the sacrifice of a bull in his honor. The maenads tear apart bulls in the frenzy of their *sparagmos* (ritual rending of animals) in the First Messenger's speech; and Pentheus is himself torn apart as a young bull-calf dedicated to the god (1340) in the *sparagmos* that ends his life, a rite to which a bull leads the way (1314). See also below on lines 717–19.

129–31 *a crown of snakes . . . and braid them through their hair* Greek vases depicting Dionysiac scenes in the fifth century often show maenads handling snakes, and the practice reappears in the description of the Theban maenads in their revel on Kithairon in 804. Here as elsewhere Euripides draws on Dionysiac imagery generally familiar to his audience. In 1017 the chorus prays to Dionysos to appear in the form of a "snake with many heads."

141 *violent fennel-rods* The unusual epithet suggests the dangerous side of the Dionysiac worship that will appear later; compare *the fennel-rod of Hades*, 1312–13, and see the note on that passage below. The combination of violence and holiness belongs to the paradoxical mixture of gentleness and terror in the god; see 979–80 and the note on that passage, below. Pentheus himself uses this same word (violence [*hubris*] in his vehement attack on the cult (288, 893), so that the recurrence of the word may also indicate the massive reversal of power in the course of the play. See below on 605–6.

142–43 *the whole earth / Will dance* A characteristically Dionysiac expression of the fusion between humankind and nature in this cult. It is exemplified in the maenads' behavior in the First Messenger's speech (804–17), where *all the mountain* and its wild inhabitants join in the Bacchic dance (833–35).

143–44 *when Bromios leads / Worshipers* A controversial and much discussed passage. We have translated the most widely accepted emendation of the unmetrical reading of the manuscripts. An alternative and less likely emendation of the text would give the sense, *whoever leads the sacred band is Bromios* and so would make the leader an incarnation of Dionysos; but here, as in 166–67 below, the reference is probably to Dionysos himself, as Bromios, the Thunderer, leading the maenads.

149–61 *Koúretês . . . birth of Zeus . . . Korybantês . . . Rhea* An etiological myth to explain how Dionysos comes to be worshiped with the exciting sounds of the flutes and drums that belong to the cult of the Phrygian mother-goddess Kybelé or Rhea. The Kouretes (attendants of Rhea) and Korybantes (attendants of Kybelé) are distinct groups and belong to different cults, but Euripides fuses them here as part of his identification of Rhea and Kybelé. In the myth of Zeus' birth, to which Euripides here refers, the Kourétes drown out the cries of the infant Zeus whom Rhea has hidden away in a cave on Crete in order to protect him from being swallowed by his father, Kronos (see Hesiod, *Theogony* 459–500). Hence they are later associated with initiatiory rites for young men. The *ecstatic satyrs* (163) are the regular attendants of Dionysos and appear frequently in Dionysiac scenes on the vases. In their part-equine attributes (horses' ears, tails, and hooves) and uninhibited appetites for wine, play, and sex, they embody the release of animal energies in Dionysiac rites. Euripides may also be alluding indirectly to the story of Rhea-Kybelé's purification of Dionysos from the madness with which the ever-vengeful Hera afflicted him, see Apollodorus, *Library of Mythology* 3.5.1.

164 *every other year* In Thebes and other cities, the maenadic rites of Dionysos, that is, the procession of the women celebrants on the mountain (the *oreibasia*), occur in midwinter of alternate years.

167–71 *throws / Himself to the ground . . . eating raw the flesh* Euripides here refers to the ritual *ōmophagia* (literally, raw-eating) in which Dionysos leads his maenads to hunt wild animals (most commonly fawns or felines) on the mountain and then tear apart and devour the raw flesh. There has been considerable controversy about the opening lines of this epode. Some interpreters think that the reference is to the god himself falling upon the hunted animal. For such a scene Roux compares Herakles falling upon a stag on a metope of the Treasury of the Athenians at Delphi at the beginning of the fifth century B.C.E.: illustration in Franz Brommer, *Heracles* (1979), trans. S. J. Schwarz (New Rochelle, N.Y., 1996), plate 8. Others have taken the reference to be to the worshiper falling to the ground either in ecstasy or exhaustion or in a trance (Dodds), or in expectation of the god's epiphany (Seaford 1996). The most likely text of the passage seems to indicate Dionysos. If these masculine forms are taken (as they sometimes are) as a generic reference to any worshiper, they are awkward for a ritual celebrated by an all-female band of bacchants.

189–90 *pride of gold- / Giving Mount Tmolos* We follow Diggle and others in reading the nominative, *khlida*, in apposition with *Bakkhants* rather than the dative form given in the manuscripts. For the locale see above, on 17–23.

198–99 *to the mountain, / To the mountain* With most interpreters, we assume that the chorus' direct quotation of Dionysos' words end here. Thus the doubled *Onward, Bakkhai* of his opening is symmetrical with the doubled *to the mountain* of his ending.

203–47 This scene between Kadmos and Teiresias has been variously interpreted. It is the first demonstration of the power of Dionysos in Thebes, but it also seems to have humorous touches. The closest parallel in Euripides' work is the miraculous rejuvenation of Herakles' companion Iolaos in the *Children of Herakles (Herakleidai)*. There, however, the rejuvenation actually takes place, whereas here the two old men go tottering off to the mountain holding one another up and afraid of falling (430–31). Interpreters remain divided about the scene's possible humor. Among the incongruities is the suggestion of male bacchants, carrying the thyrsos and wearing the fawn skin (see 209–10, 289–92), although men do participate in other aspects of Dionysos' cult. The scene may be a partly serious and partly comic anticipation of Pentheus' dressing as a maenad, with its tragic results. He too will insist on being the *only man* to undertake such a task, but in the sense of being a scapegoat-victim punished by the god, not a celebrant (1096–97). On the serious side, Dionysos often rejuvenates his worshipers, notably in Aristophanes' *Frogs* 345–48, where the old men in a procession in honor of the Eleusinian Dionysos, Iakkhos, "shake off the pains of old age and their aged years." See below, on 229.

203–4 *Kadmos . . . who left . . . Sidon* Kadmos left his Phoenician homeland in search of his sister, Europa (carried off by Zeus in the guise of a bull) and came to the site of Thebes, which he founded after killing the dragon-snake that guarded the spring of Dirké. As a culture hero, he is also said to have brought the Phoenician alphabet to Greece—a role reversed at the end of the play in his transformation into a serpent that leads a barbarian army against Greece. See Introduction, p. 28.

213 *wise man's wise voice* This is the play's first reference to wisdom (*sophia*), which becomes a major theme. *Sophia* also means the cleverness or rationalism of those who resist Dionysos and so contrasts with the god's deeper wisdom. It is used pejoratively on both sides in the sense of merely clever or tricky. In its profounder, ethical sense it raises the

questions of who is wise, the god or his mortal opponent, what wisdom is, and what kind of wisdom Dionysos and his cult offer.

215–16 *our Dionysos, / A god revealed now to mortals* This line is generally considered a later interpolation, modeled on line 979.

229 *lead the other like a child to school* a pun on the word *paidagôgos* (literally leader of a child [*pais* = child]), the aged attendant (usually a slave) who looks after the master's young male children in the house, as at the beginning of Euripides' *Medea*. The wordplay is part of the humorous undercurrent in the whole scene, but there is a serious side too in its implications for Dionysos' demand for universal worship (*no distinction between the young and old,* 244) and his cultic rejuvenation of his worshipers (see above on 203–47).

231–32 *Are we the only ones . . . Yes—only we have any sense* "Have any sense" in 232 anticipates the many inversions of sanity and madness in the play and the question of what is *wisdom* or *self-control* (*sophia* or *sôphrosynê*); see above, on 213. These lines (among others) indicate that all of Thebes and not just the royal family is implicated in the rejection of Dionysos: see, e.g., 53–55, 68–70, 896–900, 1172–73, 1456. While the Theban women are punished by becoming maenads, the men are kept in the background, perhaps because the main axes of conflict are between the strange new arrival and the rigid, authoritarian king and between male control and (supposed) female subjection and constraint.

236–37 *we don't engage / In sophistries* Another controversial passage. Euripides is alluding to the Sophists, traveling lecturers and professional speakers who taught techniques of argumentation and developed rationalistic critiques of moral behavior. The passage has puzzled interpreters because Teiresias here seems to be rejecting the kind of rationalistic skepticism or agnosticism characteristic of many of the Sophists, whereas he himself adopts sophistic rationalism in his interpretation of Dionysos in 320–54. The contradiction may be part of a parody in the presentation of Teiresias; or one or more lines may have dropped out around 236–37. Some interpreters have emended the text or reassigned the lines to Kadmos; others have suspected that the passage is the work of a later interpolator. If we keep the text of the manuscripts, the most likely view is that Teiresias is not aware of the contradiction and (as seems to have been the case with many of the Sophists) uses his rational argumentation to support what he sees as the established institutions. Read in terms of the action of the play, his rationalistic optimism will prove to be inadequate to grasp the complexities and contradictions of Dionysos.

Of the Sophists the best known are Protagoras, Gorgias, Prodikos, Hippias, and Thrasymakhos; and many of them appear as Socrates' interlocutors in the dialogues of Plato. Among the many subjects they discussed is the relation between traditional social practices (*nomoi*, also translated customs, laws) and nature (*physis*). See Introduction, pp. 13–15. The suggestion made in several odes (especially 1025–27) that tradition and nature coincide in Dionysiac cult is perhaps also in the background here in the hint that these "traditions of our fathers" are timeless and so also rooted in "nature," not inventions of a specific historical moment. The invocation of timeless tradition for a new god seems odd, but the third stasimon also argues for the reconciliation of Dionysiac cult and timeless nature (1018–27). Euripides may be implying that Dionysos' worship fulfills a timeless need that mortals have always had and so belongs to *physis* (nature), even though it arrives in Greece only at a specific historical moment.

239 *overthrown by argument* Refers to a lost work by the Sophist Protagoras (active about 450–420 B.C.E.), the Argument-Overthrowers (*Kataballontes Logoi*), which may have dealt with the possibility of making a good case for both sides of a debate.

259 *Dionysos — whoever he may be* The expression "whoever he may be" is a common ritual formula expressing piety and reverence toward a god, whose exact title and attributes may not be known. In the mouth of Pentheus, the phrase has the opposite meaning, as he is so scornful of Dionysos' divinity. It carries a certain irony, therefore, especially when it recurs, with its more usual reverent overtones, in the speech of the First Messenger: "this god, whoever he may be" (882).

267–69 *Ino . . . Aktaion* These details of Pentheus' family are intrusive here and are probably a later interpolation, made up from references later in the play. For Aktaion see below on 398–99.

280–81 *I'll cut his head / Off of his body* Euripides loses no time in depicting Pentheus' violent and impulsive character. The threat turns back against him later.

296–301 *Teiresias, . . . white hair did not protect you* A king's threats against an aged prophet and accusations of venality are attributes of the "stage tyrant" and are familiar from the encounters between Creon and Teiresias and Oedipus and Teiresias in Sophocles' *Antigone* and *Oedipus Tyrannus*, respectively. For an early example see Homer, *Odyssey* 2.184–93.

307–10 *What sacrilege . . . bring shame on all your kin* The chorus's response is in line with traditional Greek values and may well have the audience's sympathy at this point. The chorus depict the tyrannical young king as disrespectful of both the gods and the family.

311–16 *It's no great task to speak well . . . good at speaking . . . A bad citizen* Teiresias begins with familiar rhetorical motifs that call attention to the Sophistic elements in his speech.

320–21 *Listen to me . . . two great first things* Teiresias again draws on contemporary arguments characteristic of the Sophistic movement. He seems to be alluding particularly to the Sophist Prodikos, who explained the origins of religion as an allegorical divinization of forces or principles useful for human life (here the blessings of grain and wine). The extreme intellectualism of Teiresias' defense of Dionysos may be intended to suggest the failure of such rationalism to grasp the essential nature of Dionysos and his cult. See above on 236–37.

335–50 *his birth / From Zeus's thigh* In the manner of the Sophists, Teiresias uses etymology to rationalize the story that Zeus saved the infant Dionysos by sewing him up in his thigh. He relies on a three-way pun (hard to render into English) between *mêros*, (thigh), *meros* ("piece" of aether, here translated as "limb"), and *ho-mêros*, hostage. Regarding the story of Dionysos being sown in Zeus's thigh (*mêros*) as too fanciful, Teiresias has Zeus break off a "piece" (*meros*) of aether to fashion into a hostage (*ho-mêros*) for Hera, who is always jealous of Zeus' children by other women. Just how we are to understand this revision is a matter of much discussion. Is Euripides just poking fun at Sophistic rationalism? Or is he suggesting Teiresias' limited grasp of what Dionysos is? Or both? See above on 236–37.

351–58 *mantic power . . . those / He maddens tell the future . . . madness* As in the preceding lines, Teiresias relies on a specious etymological argument, the association of "mantic" and "manic" power. Etymological associations of this nature are frequent in Greek literature. For a similar play on "mantic" and "manic" see Plato, *Phaedrus* 244b-c.

354–57 *his share / Of Ares too . . . touched their spears* The description of Dionysos' martial potential (Ares is the god of war) may hint at the maenads' defeat of warriors armed with spears later and Pentheus' failure to carry through a contest of arms against Dionysos' cult.

359–62 *heights / Of Delphi . . . between the two tall peaks* The reference is to the two crags of Mount Parnassus known as the Phaidriades (the Gleaming Rocks) just above the sanctuary of Apollo at Delphi, where Dionysos held sway during the winter, while Apollo was absent. The place is a famous site of maenadic revels. See Sophocles, *Antigone* 1126–30.

371–72 *for modesty / With respect to everything* This verse is omitted in a quotation of this passage in late antiquity and is probably interpolated. It bears a suspicious resemblance to *Hippolytus* 80.

385–86 *No drug can cure your sickness* The antithesis here seems rather artificial, and (if the text is correct) the awkwardness may be due to an attempt to make a rhetorical point. Teiresias seems to be saying that Pentheus' madness must be due to (harmful) drugs but at the same time is beyond healing by medicine. There is a play on the double sense of *pharmakon* as both poisonous and medicinal drug.

387–88 *do not shame Apollo . . . praise for Bromios* The chorus's reply indicates how easily a polytheistic religion accommodates different divinities. There is no trace here of the division between Apollo and Dionysos developed in Nietzsche's *The Birth of Tragedy*.

396–98 *he is Semelé's son . . . all our clan is honored* Kadmos adduces another, more practical reason for accepting Dionysos' worship, namely the honor that accrues to the royal family from this connection to a god.

398–99 *You know how / Aktaion ended* Aktaion, cousin to Pentheus (and to Dionysos), is torn apart by his own hounds because he insults Artemis, goddess of the wild and the hunt. In this version the insult consists in boasting of his superiority in the hunt. In the version told by Ovid, *Metamorphoses* (3.138–252), and probably alluded to by Callimachus in his account of the blinding of Teiresias after seeing Athena in her bath (*Hymn* 5.109), the insult consists in accidentally seeing the goddess naked while she is bathing in a forest pool. She then transforms him into a stag, and he is hunted down and killed by his hounds. In another version his offense is the wooing of Semelé (Apollodorus, *Library of Mythology* 3.4.4). Kadmos' warning about Aktaion is fulfilled in the close parallelism of the deaths of the two young men: they meet their death in the same part of Kithairon, and both are torn apart by wild creatures that have been part of their familiar, domestic life, Pentheus by his mother and aunts turned to raging wild women, Aktaion by his own hounds who turn against him (see 1385 and 1452). The Aktaion myth was well known to Euripides' audience. It is represented on a number of vases in the mid fifth century and on a metope from temple C at Selinus (Selinunte) in Sicily, also from the mid-fifth century.

409–413 *Quickly, go . . . Throw his holy ribbands to the wind* For similar angry threats against a prophet compare the passages from Sophocles' *Antigone* and *Oedipus Tyrannus* cited above, on 296–301. Even so, the threats indicate a shocking impiety on Pentheus' part and prepare us for the divine vengeance.

412 *Pile everything together in one heap* The phrase "in one heap" *anô katô*, literally "up and down," recurs twice later to describe Dionysos' own violence of revenge against his adversary: first in the destruction of his palace in 700, "to pile it upside down in a heap," and then in the enraged Theban bacchants' attack on the villages of Pentheus' kingdom "(plundered Hysiai / And Erythrai and turned them upside down," 862–63). It is as if Pentheus calls forth the only side of Dionysos that he can perceive, an unleashing of chaotic, destructive violence.

420 *death by stoning* Having threatened the Stranger with decapitation in 280, Pentheus now threatens him with this punishment that is reserved for particularly heinous crimes, particularly sacrilege or kin murder (the former is probably intended here). The threat once more emphasizes Pentheus' violence and lack of self-control. In both cases the threats recoil upon Pentheus himself: he is to be decapitated and he will be pelted with stones by the maenads for a sacrilegious intrusion upon their rites (1240–41).

429–31 *Help me stay on my feet* Some have seen a touch of humor in these two doddering elders supporting one another as they stagger up the mountainside in Bacchic dress (see above on 203–47); yet more serious issues are also involved. Teiresias' self-consciousness of the feebleness of his years here in 430–31 contrasts with Kadmos' exuberant forgetting of old age at the beginning of the scene. The end of the play brings a more tragic contrast between old age and Dionysiac exuberance: see 1410–11, 1502, 1585, and Introduction, p. 30.

433 *Pentheus . . . repent* Here, as in several other places, Euripides plays on the name
Pentheus and the Greek noun *penthos* (grief). See also 594, 962–63,
1402–3.

436–515 *First stasimon (second ode)* Invoking the personification of Holiness or Pu-
rity, the chorus reacts to Pentheus' violence in the preceding scene by
continuing to depict him as an impious enemy of the god on the one
hand and by emphasizing the peace, beauty, festivity, and abundance
of Dionysiac worship on the other hand. The invocation of Aphrodite,
the Graces, and the gods of love and desire (478–96) in an ode to
Holiness contrasts sharply with Pentheus' accusations of lubriciousness
in Dionysos' cult and once more emphasizes its benign, innocent aspects. The far-flung geography, from Egypt and Cyprus to Pieria and
Olympus in northern Greece, like the rivers of Macedonia in the next
ode (665–70), once more underline the universality of the god and the
wide acceptance that awaits his worship in Greece. The motif of longing for a remote place of peace and beauty in the second strophe recurs
elsewhere in Euripides, notably in the "escape odes" of *Hippolytus*
(732–75) and *Helen* (1451–1511).

482–85 *Paphos . . . rainless river* Another controversial passage. If the text is right,
Euripides is alluding to a belief that the waters of the Nile somehow
fertilize Aphrodite's island of Cyprus, where her celebrated shrine at
Paphos is located. Some editors emend "Paphos" to "Pharos," a small
island off the coast of Egypt mentioned from the *Odyssey* on. Yet the
erotic associations of Aphrodite's Cyprus so emphatically placed at the
opening of the strophe strongly favor the manuscript reading, Paphos.
For other editors, however, it is this opening reference to Cyprus that
corrupted an allegedly original Pharos to Paphos.

501 *To the rich and poor alike* Euripides here emphasizes the egalitarian, democratic
aspect of Dionysos, who is traditionally associated with the people
rather than the aristocrats. The ode ends with the same sentiment in
the reference to *simple, ordinary people* in 514–15.

537 *Untie his hands* The manuscripts here read, *You are mad*, which a later hand
in the Palatinus corrected to *take hold* or *seize* (probably after 589).
Attempts to maintain the manuscript reading are unconvincing, and
with Dodds, Diggle, and Seaford we accept the emendation.

547–48 *Mount Tmolos, thick with flowers . . . makes a circle* It is characteristic of the
Dionysiac Stranger that he thinks of the flowers on the mountain

and not of the gold for which it is famous. Pentheus, on the other hand, associates the mountain with the encirclement or enclosure of its neighboring city, Sardis, the capital of Lydia. See above on 189–90.

548–94 This taut scene of line-by-line exchange (or *stichomythia*) is full of tragic ironies as Euripides plays on the god's presence in mortal guise (see especially 563–64, 586–88, 606–7). As Seaford suggests, there are probably references to the language used in the initiatory ceremonies of the Dionysiac mysteries. The scene has a pendant in the analogous exchanges later in which the Stranger leads Pentheus into a more sinister initiation to Dionysiac worship, 919–961 and 920–1105.

584 *The god himself will set me free* Allusion to Dionysos' cult title, Lysios, he who looses or releases, whether from the cares and tribulations of life or from sufferings in the underworld.

601 *household slaves working at looms* Pentheus would reassert the male control over the women of the household that is suspended when they leave the looms (and the house) for the Dionysiac procession to the mountain. Working at the loom is the traditional occupation of women in the household and the sign of the obedient, industrious wife. According to the parodos the madness sent by Dionysos has driven the women of Thebes away from their looms (146–48).

605–6 *will chase you down and then / Exact his compensation for your insults* The Stranger's warnings of punishment for Pentheus' insults (*hubrismata*) harks back to the chorus's warning in the previous ode (444) and of course foreshadows his doom. The warning now comes from the god himself (in his guise of the Lydian Stranger). The word *hubris* in both these passage implies outrageous behavior that violates the rights and honor of another person. Both sides make accusations of *hubris* against the other throughout the play (e.g. 288, 895 by Pentheus; 444, 606, 651, 714, 1564 by Dionysos or the Chorus). Kadmos' acknowledgment of Pentheus' "insult" in 1458 is perhaps an intentional echo of Pentheus' accusation of the god in 288.

608–70 *Second stasimon (third ode)* As in the preceding ode, the chorus emphasizes the joyful, and musical side of Dionysiac worship, especially in the last strophe (652–70), where fertilizing water takes up the themes of 482–85 but also harks back to the role of the saving water of the Theban spring of Dirké at the ode's beginning (608–11). Yet the chorus's warnings against Pentheus for his insults (*hubris*, 651) also become sharper

(630–51), leading directly into the god's answer to their appeal in the so-called Palace Miracle that follows.

610–11 *you took into / Your waters* The washing of the infant Dionysos by nymphs or by his nurses occurs elsewhere, but Euripides is the only extant source for washing him in Dirké's water. Possibly he is drawing on Aeschylus' lost play, *Semelé* or *The Water Carriers*, which may have included an account of Dionysos' fiery birth; see above, on 11–12.

616 *Dithyrambos* Euripides here refers to an ancient and popular (but erroneous) etymology of the word from *dis-*, twice, and *thura*, door or gate: as if the twice-born god is he who "comes twice to the gates" (of birth).

630 The manuscripts have the words "What rage, what rage" at the beginning of this antistrophe. They can be construed grammatically as the direct object of "reveal" ("What rage does Pentheus reveal, he the spawn of the Earth," etc.), but metrical considerations tell against them, and with Diggle and others we regard them as spurious.

630–38 *Pentheus, the spawn / Of earth itself . . . Ekhion as a monster . . . battles the gods* As the offspring of a serpent and of the earth, Pentheus' father, Ekhion, is a monster (at least in the chorus's eyes), and his name too has serpentine associations (cf. *ekhidna*, viper). The chorus here suggests that the monstrosity of this earthborn father continues in the son. The children of Earth, like the Giants mentioned here or primordial creatures like the ancient monster Typhoeus, are figures of disorder who combat the Olympian gods; and so the chorus uses them as a model for Pentheus' hostility to Dionysos. In 309–10 the chorus mentioned Pentheus' ancestry without the pejorative tone here. The positions harden on both sides.

652 *Mount Nysa* Of the various locations given in antiquity for this holy mountain of Dionysos, Thrace in northern Greece would perhaps be the most appropriate to this context. Along with Olympus, Parnassus, and the local Mount Kithairon, Nysa is invoked as a place for the Dionysiac *oreibasia* — the maenads' procession on the mountain.

658–60 *Orpheus . . . listening trees . . . listening beasts* In his music that reaches across the boundaries between the human and natural worlds, Orpheus has close associations with Dionysos. In Aeschylus' lost play, the *Bassarids*, set in northern Greece, he is torn apart by Thracian maenads in a distinctly Dionysiac scenario. He comes to be regarded as the mythical founder of the Orphic mysteries, in which Dionysos plays a central role. Here his power of song is also relevant to the sympathy between humankind and the natural world in the ecstasy of Dionysiac worship. See 804–17, 833–35.

665–70 *Axios . . . Lydias* The reference to these rivers of Macedonia may be due to Euripides' residence there while he was writing the play. See above on 436–515.

671–701 In this scene, known as the Palace Miracle, Dionysos intervenes miraculously with an earthquake that shakes Pentheus' palace. Simultaneously, fire blazes up from Semelé's tomb. Following directly upon the chorus, the scene is set off formally from the rest of the action by the excited meters of the chorus's lyrical dialogue with Dionysos, whose offstage voice is heard invoking the goddess of earthquake for the destruction of the palace (680). The chorus may have divided into half-choruses or individual singers for their lyrical reponses here. The excitement continues in lively trochaic tetrameters (702–45), as Dionysos, in his disguise as the Stranger, emerges from the palace and describes the frenzy and frustration of Pentheus. The regular meter of the iambic trimeter (the usual dialogue meter) resumes only with Pentheus' return to the stage at 746.

The scene is the first of Dionysos' epiphanies in the play and the first open display of his supernatural power. As such, it marks a shift in the balance of power from the mortal to the god in the play's long central section that culminates in Pentheus' final exit for his death, dressed as a maenad and totally in the god's power, at 1105. The toppling of the palace is both a visual symbol for the collapsing authority of the king, identified with the integrity of his house, and (as in Euripides' *Herakles*) a sign of the imminent disintegration of his sanity.

How much of this scene was actually staged? The rudimentary stage machinery and stylized conventions can hardly have permitted the actual toppling of the palace, which, in any case, seems to be standing when Agaué enters before her dialogue with Kadmos at 1356. Possibly drums and violent movement by the chorus, accompanied by the excited meter of 671–701, were enough to suggest the event. The chorus's vivid "Do you see . . . Do you see" in 693–94 may imply some special scenic effects at Semelé's shrine, which was probably part of the stage set; but this too may have been left to the imagination or understood as the language of religious epiphany. Pentheus mistakenly assumes that the god's flash of fire in 721–24 means that his palace is on fire. But, even if nothing happens to the stage building, this does not mean that we should regard the shaking of the palace merely as an illusion-istic trick by the Stranger, as was suggested by interpreters early in the century, such as Gilbert Norwood (*The Riddle of the Bacchae* [Man-chester, 1908] and A. W. Verrall, *The Bacchants of Euripides and Other Essays* [Cambridge, 1910]). Euripides' audience would probably have regarded the combination of a bright light, a mysterious divine voice from an invisible source, shaking of the earth, and thunder as regular features of a god's epiphany (compare the ending of Sophocles' *Oedi-pus at Colonus* and Dionysos' epithet Bromios, "the Thunderer"). As Seaford suggests, some of these effects may be suggestive of the Dio-nysiac mysteries.

Euripides, finally, may be alluding to Aeschylus' play about Lykour-gos' resistance to Dionysos in his *Edonians*, of which a verse, quoted admiringly in the treatise *On the Sublime* 15.6 (probably of the late first century C.E. and attributed to Longinus) describes the king's palace as seized by a Dionysiac frenzy: "The palace is full of the god, the roof is in a bacchic revel." Aeschylus was known for his bold stage effects, and Euripides may be deliberately recalling his predecessor's work. The descriptive trochaic tetrameters of the following scene (702–45) are also an archaic feature of tragedy and characteristic of Aeschylus.

697 *Throw yourselves down, maenads* The only place in the play where the Lydian women of the chorus (in contrast to the maddened women of Thebes) are called maenads, which carries the suggestion of madness. The word here may be due to the intensely Dionysiac nature of the scene, but it may also subtly foreshadow the more aggressive stance of the chorus in the latter part of the play.

702 *Barbarian women* This is a somewhat odd way for the Stranger (himself a Lydian and so a "barbarian") to address his followers. He addresses them only as *Women* in 964 and calls the Theban maenads *Young women* in the epiphany of 1221. Possibly the term underlines their strangeness to Thebes and so (like *maenads* in 697, above) begins to mark their in-creasingly aggressive and adversarial relationships to the city. See below on 964–80.

706 *O greatest light of the joyful cries of the Bakkhanal* Light is a common metaphor in Greek literature for relief and salvation and so is appropriate for the joy that the chorus now feels with the return of its leader; but the close association here with Dionysiac ritual may carry associations of the god's mystery rites and their symbolism of rebirth, as at Eleusis, where the birth of the divine child Iakkhos is "accompanied by much fire."

The light may also remind us of the miracle of the epiphany that we have just witnessed. See below, on lines 729–32. The play frequently uses the word *Bakkhanal*, generally in the plural, of Dionysos' *bacchic rites* or revels (e.g., 55, 373, 827).

717–19 *found a bull . . . dripping sweat* Pentheus' sweaty wrestling with a bull in the stables of the palace anticipates his vision of the Stranger as a bull in 922 as he passes even more directly under the god's power of illusion, which is also prominent in the following lines, especially 729–32. For the recurrent motif of the bull as an epiphanic form of Dionysos throughout the play see above on 128. The panting and sweating in these lines may also carry sexual overtones; and we may recall Pentheus' suspicions of the bacchants' licentiousness at his entrance (304–6), his interest in the Stranger's sexual attractiveness in their first scene together (538–45), and the chorus's ode on Aphrodite and Cyprus, 478–96. In his heated wrestling with the bull, closely associated with male sexuality, Pentheus seems to be struggling with his own animal and sexual nature; and the god becomes an increasingly radical version of a sensual alter ego that Pentheus cannot integrate into his current self-image.

720 *completely calm* "Calm" returns repeatedly in this scene (as it does elsewhere in the play) for the contrast between the peacefulness of the benign side of Dionysos and the increasing bafflement of his mortal antagonist. See also 738–40, 751 and the Stranger's advice to Pentheus to "be calm" in 906. See also 460–65 and below on 745.

725 *To bring the river Akheloüs itself* Akheloüs is here used by metonymy for water in general, but perhaps with a touch of mocking humor directed against Pentheus' frantic and futile response to the miraculous events going on around him.

729–32 *Bromios made a phantom shape . . . shining air* The manuscripts at 730 read "light," *phôs*, which many editors emend to *phasm(a)*, phantom, apparition. "Made light" is not very natural Greek. The manuscript reading has been defended, however, as a reference to the initiatory imagery of the scene and the mystic associations of light out of darkness (so especially Seaford, and see above on 706). In line 732 a noun after "shining" has dropped out in the manuscripts; so a word must be added to fit both meter and syntax. *Aether* (pure air) is the most widely accepted supplement; other editors prefer *eidos*, (form, likeness, image).

735 *shook the buildings down—the place has all collapsed* The details of this rapid and phantasmagoric narrative are not entirely clear and possibly were not meant to be. Dionysos may be referring to his destruction of the palace shortly before (680–701) or, possibly, to the outlying buildings, the stables where Pentheus sees the bull.

739–40 *And I came out / Quite calm . . . He'll come out, now* Dionysos echoes his opening words in the play as his appearance from the palace now constitutes a new, special epiphany for his worshipers. His "calm" exit also contrasts markedly with Pentheus' excited "coming out"; gestures doubtless reinforced the contrast. The manuscripts at 739 read "leading forth maenads," which cannot be right and is generally emended to read "I came out."

742–43 *what / Can he say* Possibly an echo of Kadmos' phrase introducing Pentheus at his first entrance in 254.

744–45 *a man / Who is wise has self-control* The repetition of the key moral terms "wise" and "self-control" (*sophos* and *sôphrôn*) once more signals the contrasting views of these virtues by Pentheus and Dionysos. This combination of calm, wisdom, and self-control also harks back to the benign vision of Dionysiac worship in the first stasimon, 460–65. See above on 45–50 and 213.

746 *What terrible, strange things I've suffered* The verb here, *pepontha*, (I've suffered), may contain another play on Pentheus' name (cf. *penthos* [suffering, grief].

755–57 The interruption of the line-by-line repartee is unusual, but not unexampled (see Seaford, whose view of the text we accept). Most editors assume that a line (or more) has been lost, either after 755 (so Diggle) or after 756 (so Dodds). If such an approach is taken, we prefer Dodds's solution, which gives 756 to Pentheus (as in our text) as an ironical reply to Dionysos' statement about wine, in keeping with Pentheus' suspicions in 259–61 and 304–6, with a lacuna following 756. Line 757 would then be a response to a lost statement of Dionysos about entering or having entered Thebes.

759 *You're oh so smart, so smart* Another play on the word *sophos* (wise) and the issue of wisdom. See above on 213.

766 *glittering falls of brilliant snow still lie* Whether the reference is to fallen snow or to snowstorms is debated. At present snow does not lie on Kithairon

all year long, but it may have been cooler twenty-five hundred years ago. Snowstorms are possible during a good part of the year. Greek tragedy does not usually indicate a particular season of the year, but the reference here may be a reminder of the midwinter time of the *oreibasia*, the maenadic revel on the mountain. Seneca, *Oedipus* 808 refers to "Kithairon's snowy ridge."

783–889 The first of two long and highly detailed Messenger speeches about the Theban maenads' activities on Mount Kithairon. Its pendant, the Second Messenger's speech at 1180–1307, also ends with a generalization about Dionysos' gift to mortals. See Introduction p. 26. Both speeches present visions of a beatific calm and harmony with nature, followed by an abrupt change to violence and bloodshed, thereby showing the two faces of Dionysos.

804 *Fastening the dappled skins with snakes* See above on lines 129–31.

811–17 *Struck her thyrsos . . . honey . . . from the ivied rods* Miracles involving milk, honey, wine, and water are traditionally attributed to Dionysos and his maenads. See Plato, *Ion* 534a, "The bacchants, when they are inspired, not in their senses, draw forth honey and water from rivers." These miraculous events remind us of Dionysos' association with fertility and the liquid life and energy of nature. A miraculous dripping of honey also accompanies Dionysos' epiphany to the daughters of Minyas who resist his cult at Orkhomenos (Aelian, *Varia Historia* 3.42, and see Introduction p. 16, with note 29).

822 *These strange, miraculous events* Some editors delete this line as an interpolation based on 773, but the play's continual hammering away at these repeated "wonders" effectively depicts Pentheus' stubbornness and folly. See Introduction, p. 20.

822–23 *one / Of us, who used to wander through the town . . . good at talking* What exactly is this city-slicker doing among cowherds and shepherds on the mountain? Euripides' Messenger perhaps means to suggest a contrast between the more naive, instinctively religious, and acceptant country folk and the skeptical, worldly man of the town. By the end of the speech the Messenger clearly classes himself with the believers. Euripides may be alluding also to the pernicious effects of the demagogic politicians of late fifth-century Athens, often satirized by Aristophanes.

833–34 *And all the mountain . . . joined them* A characteristically Dionysiac fusion of the human and natural worlds. In a glorious Dionysiac ode of the

Antigone, the fifth stasimon (1115–54), Sophocles' envisages Dionysos as the chorus leader of a cosmic dance of "fire-breathing stars" (1146–54). Compare also the verse from Aeschylus' *Edonians* cited above, on 671–701 (p. 114).

847 *Pulling in two a big young heifer* With Dodds and Diggle, we accept the emendation of the eighteenth-century classicist, J. J. Reiske "pulling" (*helkousan*) in place of the manuscripts "holding" (*ekhousan*).

851–57 *ribs and hooves hurled up . . . rags of flesh / Were torn from them* The *sparagmos* (ritual dismemberment) of the cattle by the enraged maenads is another warning to Pentheus. The verb in the phrase *still dripping blood* in 853 prefigures Agaüe's description of Pentheus' mangled body in her lament over him at the end of the play ("blood-dripping limbs," a line restored on the basis of *Christus Patiens* 1471, see Appendix). Compare also 1285–88 and 1318–19.

862–63 Hysiai, Erythrai Villages on the north slope of Mount Kithairon, directly on the way to Thebes.

864 *snatched the children . . . from their homes* This maenadic activity is corroborated by the evidence of vases and some late literary evidence. It contrasts with the peaceful, nurturing actions of the women before the herdsmen's attack (789–817). At the same time, the maenads have left behind the nurture of their own infants at home and instead suckle the young of wild beasts (805–9). They thus threateningly disrupt and invert the normal restrictions and obligations of women in the Greek household.

866–73 *Stayed where they put it and never fell* The text has suffered some disruption at this point. Manuscript L breaks off at 865. The remaining manuscript, P, places the phrase "bronze and iron . . . to the black earth" after 866 and connects the metals with the maenads' plunder from the houses; but "black earth" is probably an interpolation, and "bronze and iron" probably goes with the account of the battle in 873; we have translated accordingly.

893–94 *Bakkhic violence blazes up / . . . like wildfire* Pentheus' angry comparison of the Maenads' attack to fire again points up the gap between his perceptions of Dionysos and the numinous reality of the god. Fire has been a recurrent attribute of Dionysos' miracles, first at the tomb of Semelé ("the live flame of Zeus" around her tomb, 11), then at the shaking of Pentheus' palace (692–96), later in the illusion of fire that Pentheus tries to extinguish there (722–25), and finally in the Messenger's account, shortly before Pentheus' outburst in the "blazing fire" that plays around the hair of the maenads themselves (868).

927 *Aaah!* This exclamation from the Stranger stands outside the regular meter and so calls attention to his sudden change of tactic. The disguised Dionysos now begins to establish his uncanny, quasi-hypnotic control over Pentheus.

938 *ritual robe of linen* Of Egyptian origin, linen robes seem to have funereal and initiatory associations.

946 *eager to watch maenads* The Stranger' phrase, (literally to be a *spectator* of maenads) can also apply to a dramatic performance, and is part of a pattern of self-reflexive reference to staging and dramatic illusion.

962–63 *I think that I'll go in . . . suffer your advice* These two verses are Pentheus' last, feeble protest against Dionysos' power over him. He speaks as if he still had a choice between following the Stranger's advice or going armed (i.e., leading his troops against the maenads as he was so vehement about doing in his immediate response to the Messenger's speech, 893–902). In fact, once he has begun to listen to this advice, he has already surrendered to the god's power. Line 962 also plays on the double meaning of verb *peisomai*, "I shall obey" and "I shall suffer," in the latter sense recalling the suffering or grief (*penthos*) contained in Pentheus' name. See on 433, 1402–3.

964–80 *Women! The man is heading . . . gentle* This address to the women, harking back to the address to the *barbarian women* in 702, confirms the new stage in the humiliation of Pentheus. Although the Stranger here addresses the Lydian bacchants of the chorus with privileged foreknowledge of Pentheus' death, he nevertheless does not completely abandon his disguise as the Stranger; note his address to the god in 966. His summary of the action of the rest of the play reveals how quickly Dionysos has taken control of Pentheus: within the space of some thirty lines the king changes from proud and hostile antagonist to humiliated and ridiculous victim. The dressing of Pentheus probably reflects actual Dionysiac rituals, in which men dressed in women's clothing. See Dodds on 854–55. Simultaneously, it is an ironic version of an adolescent rite of passage (that often involves temporarily dressing in the clothes of the opposite sex), a perverted initiation into the Dionysiac mysteries, the preparation of the victim for sacrifice, and the dressing of a corpse for burial (*what he'll wear / To Hades*, 976–77).

979–80 *Was born a god in full, and is / Most terrible . . . most gentle* The text and meaning of these important lines are controversial because of the problematical phrase *en telei*, which we take to mean something like "completely"—Dionysos is "in every sense a god." Diggle suggests the emendation *en merei*, in the sense "in turn," but Euripides generally uses that phrase with verbs and not in the kind of noun-copula-predicate adjective construction that we have here. Whatever the exact sense of *en telei*, the two superlatives must go closely together, and the lines must mean that Dionysos is "most terrible and most gentle to mortals." The two sides of Dionysos have been everywhere in evidence throughout the play, and it is the terrible side that we see here; but the Stranger's last word, *most gentle*, reminds us of the balance, which again becomes visible in the following ode.

981–1043 Third stasimon (fourth ode) This ode marks a turning point in the play. Its theme is divine justice (especially in the antistrophe), but it begins with a green world of wild forests that harks back to the earlier odes and to the harmony with nature shown in the First Messenger's speech. The closing epode, a general reflection on the precariousness of human happiness, touches on the motif of the blessedness and calm that the chorus numbered among Dionysos' gifts in their entering ode, but it puts Pentheus' life into the broader philosophical perspective that one expects from the chorus in Greek tragedy.

984–85 *Will I ever fling back / My head* Dionysiac vases of the fifth century often depict maenads dancing in just this pose, with the head flung back.

1002–6 repeated in 1028–32. *What is wise . . . What is beautiful is what is always loved* The text has a minor problem, but the sense is clear. The chorus asserts its pleasure in contemplating vengeance on its enemies, anticipating the more intense expression of this theme in the next ode. The "wisdom" of the gods, as the following antistrophe implies, holds the justice of such revenge. The last line, an ancient proverb, implies their recognition of the rightness of the divine vengeance that Dionysos has now set in motion against Pentheus. At the same time, of course, the play also makes us wonder about the "wisdom" and "beauty" in this vengeance. Some interpreters believe that the last line implies a negative answer to the question about the beauty of this vengeance, but that view does not fit the following antistrophe, nor does it square with the chorus's behavior in the following ode and their response to the Second Messenger.

1022–27 *It costs so little . . . comes to be through nature* The chorus here asserts the harmonious agreement of *nomos* and *physis*, (custom-law and nature), and then seems to be suggesting their further association with the divine, that is, their coming together in the worship of Dionysos. See above, on lines 236–37, and Introduction, 13–15. The syntax is very dense, and commentators offer a range of possible interpretations.

1041–43 *those whose lives are happy* The language of blessedness harks back to the chorus's opening ode (96–99), but at the point when Dionysiac worship also begins to reveal its "terrifying" side (979–80). See above, on 981–1043.

1044–1105 This scene is Pentheus' last appearance on the stage. He is now totally in the god's power and is dressed as a maenad, in striking contrast to his martial challenge to the god in the previous scene (893–902). His vision of a double sun becomes a literary commonplace for insanity in classical writers (e.g., Virgil, *Aeneid* 4.469–70). The scene has many levels of meaning. In ritual terms, it is an epiphany of the god in his bull-like form as he leads his antagonist to his doom (see 1153, 1314, and above, on 128 and 717–19). It is a "dedication" of Pentheus (1069) as a sacrifice to the god and prepares him to be a scapegoat-victim who alone will take upon himself all the ills of the community and purge them by his death (1096–99). It is a failed rite of passage by a transvestism that will turn the youth not into the adult hoplite warrior but into a scout or spy (1090–91), which is the task of the ephebe (youth between eighteen and twenty) before achieving full warrior status. And it is a sinister initiation of Pentheus into the Dionysiac mysteries, promising a "salvation" from which in fact there will be no return (1101). The scene also uses the ritual structure of procession — contest — celebratory revel (*pompê — agôn — kômos*) that is then repeated for Agauë when she enters to celebrate her "contest," the victorious "hunt" in which she has killed Pentheus. In both cases, of course, the celebratory meaning is ironically inverted: see Introduction, notes 17–18. The scene is also a remarkable piece of dramatic self-reflexivity or metatragedy in which the poet calls attention to the theater's creation of dramatic illusion by masking and dressing. More specifically still, it enacts the specific theatricality of Greek drama generally, in which male actors dressed in female garb play women's roles. Aristophanes' *Thesmophor-*

iazusae (*Women at the Thesmophoria*), produced in 411 B.C.E., shortly before Euripides left Athens, offers a comic version of this scene in an analogous plot: Euripides, accused by the women of Athens of revealing their vices, gets a relative of his to dress as a woman in order to infiltrate their sacred festival, where he is caught and (this being comedy) rescued.

1049–50 *ready / To spy on your own mother and on her troupe* The Greek word for *troupe* here, *lokhos*, can also mean "military band" (as a troop or squad of soldiers) and "ambush." These additional meanings add to the tragic ironies of the reversals, as the warrior-king is destroyed by women and in the dress of a woman rather than under arms.

1051 *You have the very form* We are reminded of Dionysos' change of his own "form" in the prologue (73).

1057 *bullified* Euripides uses an unusual word, which on its rare occurrences elsewhere in tragedy means "act like a bull," (i.e., act with bull-like savagery or look at with bull-like savagery, but not to become a bull.) The word signals the special effect of Dionysos' private epiphany in his taurine shape in a scene that is much concerned with disguise, illusion, and metamorphosis. For the ritual importance of the god's appearance as a bull see above, on 128 and 717–19.

1071 *below your ankles* Pentheus is now wearing the "full-length robes" that the Stranger described in 950.

1086–87 *Don't go destroying the shrines of nymphs . . . And the haunts of Pan* Humoring his deluded victim, the Stranger would protect these haunts of the rustic gods from a Pentheus who, even in his madness, has destructive tendencies (cf. his threats against Teiresias' seats of augury in 409–51). Pan's love of flutesong and dancing with the nymphs in wild mountainous places suggests his affinity with the maenads on their mountain revels or *oreibasia*. The *Homeric Hymn to Pan* relates that "bacchic Dionysos" took particular delight in Pan's birth when his father Hermes showed him off on Olympus (*Homeric Hymns* 19.45–46).

1103–5 *Soft delight . . . force me to be spoiled* The Greek contains a play on the word spoil (*truphê*), from a root meaning to break up, so that there is an ironic allusion to the breaking up of Pentheus in the maenadic *sparagmos* (ritual tearing apart). This last dialogue between Pentheus and the Stranger increases the emotional intensity by accelerating the line-by-line repartee into half-line exchanges, a device known as *antilabê*.

1108 *A fame that rises all the way to heaven* An ironical reference to the motif of "fame reaching to the heavens" in Homeric epic, indicating how far Pentheus falls short of the heroic ideal.

1109 *Open your arms, Agauë* The Stranger's address to Agauë, who, of course, is still offstage, marks the completion of the god's revenge. It continues the pattern of the offstage cry of Dionysos to his worshipers in the Palace Miracle (692–701) and his two addresses to them at 702 and 964. This is the last time that the god appears in disguise. When we next hear his words, they will be the direct address from the heavens, as reported in the mysterious epiphany described by the Second Messenger (1219–29).

1113–59 Fourth stasimon (fifth ode) This is the last regular ode that the chorus sings, and their mood is now dominated by the lust for bloody revenge, especially in the refrain of 1128–32 and 1148–52. As Dionysos begins to execute his punishment of Pentheus, his maenad chorus increasingly shows its murderous side.

1113 *Hounds of Fury, rush to the mountain* The chorus echo the cry of the opening ode (187, 198–99), but the mood is now totally different as the god's followers, yielding to their own rage, urge on the maddened Theban maenads much as Agauë did in the First Messenger speech ("O hounds of the chase," 839). "Hounds of Fury" (or Madness, *Lyssa*) evokes the Furies or Erinyes, dread vengeful deities of the Underworld. Fury here (in Greek Lyssa) is a fearful chthonic divinity, personification of destructive madness. In Aeschylus' lost play, *Xantriai* (*The Wool-carders*), which had a Dionysiac subject, the "goad of Fury" is invoked for the rending apart (*sparagmos*) of someone who is resisting the god, probably Pentheus. In Euripides' *Herakles* Fury is sent by Hera to drive Herakles to the homicidal rage in which he kills his wife and children and actually appears on the stage (*Herakles* 843–73).

1118 *Against this man who mimics woman* The chorus refers back to the Stranger's description of Pentheus in 975 as "a man-turned-woman," about to be led out of the town to the mountain.

1118 *from some tall pole or rocky cliff* The Greek word *skolops* (pole) is unattested elsewhere in this sense. It usually means stake or other sharp-pointed instrument and may be corrupt, a gloss or mistaken conjecture for Euripides' original word. We should recall that there is only one surviving manuscript for the play after line 865.

1125–27 *not born / From the blood of women* In its vengeful fury, the chorus demonizes Pentheus, making him the offspring of the monstrous Gorgons. The chorus had called Pentheus a monster in the second stasimon (630–38); now their outcry is fiercer. The discrepancy between the bestial antagonist that they imagine and the confused youth whom Dionysos has just led to his doom also begins to shift sympathy toward Pentheus. There is no mitigation of his impiety and folly, but his sufferings begin to appear in a different perspective as the full horror of the god's punishment emerges. This ode has an important role in that shift of perspective.

1138–43 *Him, death will not be slow to teach . . . / What is great and is clear* The text of this passage has many uncertainties; our translation follows Dodds, but with no great confidence.

1143–52 *what leads us . . . to be holy / And reverent . . . Earthborn offspring!* The contradictions in this chorus are strongly marked here. The chorus hark back to the motifs of Dionysiac wisdom, calm, and holiness in the previous odes but then repeat their call for bloody, throat-slitting revenge in the refrain. They conclude with a prayer for a Dionysiac epiphany, but the god is to appear in the bestial and aggressive forms of bull, many-headed snake, fiery lion, and hunter. The maenads are a deadly herd, beneath whom Pentheus will fall; and the metaphor emphasizes the collective emotion of the *thiasos*, the band of devotees. We may also be reminded of Dionysos as leader of the maenads in the *oreibasia*, the mountain revel, "throwing himself" (literally, falling) upon the hunted prey in the first ode (167–68); and yet the contrast between this ode and that first ode is striking. At the same time the god, in his calm remoteness, has a "laughing face," which now makes us understand the sinister power behind the laughter of the Stranger when he is led before Pentheus for the first time in 516.

1160–61 *O house . . . of that patriarch of Sidon.* This honorific reference to the founding of the city and the Planted Men offers a perspective on Thebes' origins very different from that of the chorus in the previous ode (1125–27). After line 1164, "Although I am your slave—but even so!," the manuscript contains the additional line "For decent slaves must bear the sorrows of their masters' fate," which, with most editors, we regard as a later interpolation, based on *Medea* 54. Some editors would excise also the preceding two lines, 1161–62, which mention Kadmos' Phoenician origins and his foundation of Thebes; but the reference to the "house" alone, without a proper name, seems too bare. In contrast to the First Messenger, who addressed Pentheus, the Second Messenger addresses only the "house" of Kadmos, not Kadmos himself, who will enter only later. His audience is only the Lydian maenads of the chorus, hostile to that house, and they will receive the catastrophic news with the rejoicing that unsettles this Messenger.

1180–1307 *Second Messenger's speech* In the structure of the play this long narrative is symmetrical with the First Messenger's speech, but now the destructive side of the maenads predominates, and their calm and peaceful activities receive only a brief description (1191–96). The intruder into the maenads' rites is now the king himself, not the herdsmen, and the result is a far more deadly and horrible *sparagmos*: the rending of human flesh and not just of cattle. The landscape too is correspondingly harsher (1189–90).

1207–9 *wheel-curve* the text and meaning of this comparison have been much discussed. Some scholars have thought the reference to be to a kind of lathe.

1219–21 *the Stranger disappeared, and a voice . . . Cried out* The Stranger of the first two-thirds of the play is now replaced by the full divine power of Dionysos, made manifest by the voice from the sky, see below on 1224–33. The details of this epiphany have close resemblances to the divine summoning of Oedipus at the end of Sophocles' *Oedipus at Colonus* (1621–30), Sophocles' last play, written not long after the *Bakkhai*. These resemblances may be due to literary convention, but it is possible, as Dodds suggests, that Sophocles might have read an advance copy of the *Bakkhai* in late 407 or early 406 B.C.E.

1221–22 *the man / Who makes a mockery* The mockery (or laughter) now is wholly on Dionysos' side, see 521 and 1156, and above, on 1143–52.

1224–33 *as the voice proclaimed . . . Dionysos' voice* This is the decisive epiphany of Dionysos and the answer to the chorus's prayer at the end of the previous ode (1153–59). The sudden silence, bright light, and voice from the heavens are all signs of the god's supernatural presence. Compare the earthquake, offstage voice, and flash of light in the Palace Miracle, 690–707. See above, on 671–701.

1233–34 With Dodds, Diggle, and many editors we bracket these lines as a later interpolation.

1239–96 The narrative of Pentheus' death. This extraordinary passage, a detailed description of a Dionysiac ritual rending (or *sparagmos*), is the climax of Dionysos' vengeance and of the homicidal insanity that he unleashes against his adversary. It is dense with ritual implications and ironic inversions of ritual. Pentheus is simultaneously a maenad and a victim of maenads, a scapegoat-victim, a hunted beast, a "young bull-calf" (see 1340) and a wild lion (see 1295, 1351), and most spectacularly perhaps a surreal thyrsos brandished in a maenadic procession on the mountain, where his head will replace the ivy cluster at the tip of the fennel-stalk (1140–41): see Christine M. Kalke, "The Making of a Thyrsus," *American Journal of Philology* 106 (1985), 409–26. As a wild lion, he evokes the scenes on Dionysiac vases, where ecstatic maenads tear apart wild felines and carry their body parts. There are a number of vases that represent the *sparagmos* of Pentheus, as early as the late sixth century B.C.E.: see Carpenter, *Dionysiac Imagery* (Introduction, note 6), 116–17, with plates 46–47. It would be interesting to know how much Euripides' account owes to Aeschylus' lost *Pentheus*.

1250 *Striking with oak branches like thunderbolts* The text and meaning of this line are controversial. The verb, strike as with a thunderbolt, has Dionysiac associations (compare Dionysos' epithet, Bromios, the Thunderer, and the role of thunder and lightning at his birth), and so it is suggestive of the supernatural power that the god has given his maenads in their irresistible violence against Pentheus. We have adopted an emendation (accepted also by Seaford) that makes the maenads use these branches as levers to uproot the tall fir tree in which Pentheus is trapped. The manuscript, supported by a papyrus fragment, has the oak branches as the direct object, in the accusative case, (i.e., "striking the oaken branches as if with thunder," which Dodds accepts. If, with Dodds, we keep the transmitted text, the reference is perhaps to the role of oak in the bacchic ritual, as in the opening ode, where fir and oak are combined (*consecrate / Yourselves as Bakkhai with / Sprays of oak and pine!* 136–38; cf. also 810, where the maenads crowned themselves with ivy, oak leaves, vines). But the manuscript reading makes it hard to connect whatever the maenads are doing with the goal of their efforts at this moment of the narrative.

1254 *this tree-climbing beast* Pentheus now appears to the maenads as one of those animals that maenads hunt down and tear apart. The reversal of human and bestial, hunter and hunted pervades the play and becomes even stronger with Agauë's appearance in the next scene. Compare also the First Messenger's speech, 839–43, and the end of the previous ode, 1156–59. The god too appears as both the hunter and the beast.

1255–56 *revealing to anyone / The secret dances of the god* In contrast to these secret rites on the mountain, the Lydian maenads' procession through the city in the opening ode, though requiring holy silence, is visible to all. Pentheus' disguise in order to spy on the Theban maenads in 1089–91 emphasizes the secrecy. Like other mysteries, they are forbidden to the profane. Aristophanes' *Thesmophoriazusae* offers a comic analogy: see above, on 1044–1105. Early in the play, on the other hand, Kadmos and Teiresias will go to the mountain to honor the god, but nothing is said of their joining the women in their maenadic dances (see above, on 231–32).

1283 *raising the war-cry of their triumph* The maenads' cry is that of the male warrior in martial victory, which continues the pervasive inversion of gender roles. Diggle emends the manuscript text to read *ôloluzon*, which refers to the distinctively female cry, at ritual occasions, especially the sacrifice of an animal (see Dodds on line 24). For a good defense of the manuscript text see Seaford.

1312–13 *the fennel-rod of Hades, / The thyrsos that is the warrant of his death* A controversial passage that has been much emended and that Diggle still marks as corrupt. The manuscript reading, "trusty Hades," makes little sense, but the modern emendation "pledge of Hades" (involving the change of a single letter in the Greek) is now confirmed by a papyrus fragment of the fifth century C.E. and is widely accepted by editors. The thyrsos is a "pledge of Hades" in the sense that it is the token that will admit Pentheus to Hades, realm of death, in a perverted and destructive form of initiatory passage to the underworld. Hence our translation, "warrant of his death."

1314 *a bull was in command!* Compare Pentheus' vision of the Stranger as a bull as he leads him to the mountain in 1054–57 and his wrestling with the bull in the palace in 717–18.

1316–17 *hymn of triumph . . . lamentation* This song, which prepares for Agauë's entrance with Pentheus' head, is a perverted form of the ritual pattern of procession — contest — revel: see above, on 1044–1105. In the play's pervasive reversal of gender roles, the mother is the victorious athlete, hunter, and leader of a revel (*kômos*), all exclusively masculine activities. Simultaneously, victory song fuses with funerary dirge, for the triumphant line-by-line antiphonal responsion between the women of the chorus and Agauë in what follows (1323–55) is also evocative of female funerary lament.

1318–19 *to plunge her hand in the blood / Of her child* the text of this passage has been much discussed. With Dodds, we adopt the emendation of the nineteenth-century classicist, Adolf Kirchhof (*balein*), which makes the expression parallel to that of *Medea* 1283.

1324–26 *Because . . . for this house, we bring in a blessèd hunt, / A fresh-cut tendril* In 1292–93 the Messenger described Agauë as placing the head on the tip of her thyrsos; now, as she appears on the stage for the first time, she carries it in her arms, thereby fulfilling the Stranger's promise to Pentheus in 1103–4. This entrance ranks with that of the blinded Oedipus in Sophocles' *Oedipus Tyrannus* as one of one of the most powerful and shocking visual spectacles of the Greek theater. The "fresh-cut tendril" belongs to the Dionysiac imagery of the vital energies of nature; but there is deep tragic irony in the mad Agauë's confusion of the ivy-like curling plant with the curling hair of the captured beast. See on 1340–42, below. For Plutarch's account of the performance of this scene with the head of Crassus at the Parthian court see the Introduction, p. 6. As the tragedies in Euripides' time were performed by three main actors (all male), presumably the actor who played Pentheus now took the role of Agauë. The head of Pentheus that she/he carries is perhaps the mask that this actor had just worn in that role, or else closely resembles it, stained, perhaps, to represent its decapitated state.

1329–30 *This young creature, / As you see* A phrase has dropped out of the manuscript, perhaps referring to Pentheus as looking like a young lion.

1339 *So share this feast* An allusion to the *ômophagia*, the maenads' devouring of their hunted prey raw on the mountain. The half-line leaves open the horrible possibility that the maenads actually devoured some of Pentheus' body. When Agauë returns to Thebes and is still mad, she repeatedly urges Kadmos to hold a feast (1400, 1406), as if the hunted beast were not a lion (see 1329–30, 1439 or 1444) but an animal more appropriate for a feast, like the "young bull-calf" of 1340–42 (below) — a deliberate vacillation between Pentheus as sacrificial victim (like a bull) and as hunted wild beast: see my *Dionysiac Poetics* (Introduction, note 4), 40–45.

1340–42 *This young bull-calf . . . his delicate crest of hair, like a helmet* Pentheus' head appears to Agaüe confusedly as that of both a young bull and a lion (1350; see also 1439, 1444)). The reference to the crest (for which Euripides here uses the usual Greek word for helmet) may also suggest Pentheus' failure to achieve the warrior status for which he was arming himself at the moment when he fell under the Stranger's spell (926, 963).

1358–70 On the gender reversals in Agaüe's delusion of herself see above on 1316–17.

1376–77 *scattered . . . in thick / Impenetrable woods* The line is suspect and has been deleted by some editors, but we believe it to be genuine.

1385 *Aktaion* See above on 398–99.

1397 *the prize for prowess* The reference here is to the usual prize for valor (*aristeia*) awarded to the best warrior—another inversion of gender roles in Agaüe's madness. See above on 1283, 1316–17, 1358–70.

1399–1400 *call your friends / To feast, for you are blessèd, blessèd* On the horror and ambiguity of this feasting see above, on 1339. The repeated blessèd echoes the beatitudes of the Lydian worshipers in their opening song (97) but with cruel irony as we now see the dark side of Dionysiac ecstasy.

1402–3 *O grief . . . pitiable hands* If the lines are genuine, grief (*penthos*) contains another play on Pentheus' name. Editors have doubted the authenticity of the lines, largely because of the syntactical irregularity in 1402. With Dodds and others, we believe the lines to be genuine, except for the second half of 1402, which means something like "on which I cannot look," and for syntactical reasons is probably to be considered corrupt. Possibly a line or two has dropped out of the manuscript at this point.

1415–16 *fight / Against divinity* Agaüe now echoes Dionysos' warning description of Pentheus in the prologue (60).

1425–41 *look up . . . at the sky . . . What's this I'm holding in my hands?* This scene has been compared to a psychotherapeutic intervention. See Introduction, note 43. Living in Macedonia may have given Euripides some experience of how maenads and others in ecstatic states were brought back to normal consciousness.

1461 On the problem of the lacunas in the text here and in 1512 see the Appendix. We have supplied Agauë's lament as she pieces together Pentheus' body (a scene known as the *Compositio Membrorum*) from the (probably late) Byzantine play, the *Christus Patiens*, a dramatic version of the Passion of Christ which draws heavily on this and other Euripidean plays.

1482–1509 Following upon Agauë's lament (as we suppose) in the gap after 1461, Kadmos now makes his lament over the body. He emphasizes the loss to the house as a whole and, as befits a former king, puts greater emphasis on the public world, Pentheus' defense of his grandfather's honor and dignity in the city. This lament of an aged king over a grandson who (it would seem) is the last male survivor of the house (1487–89) should be compared with Peleus' lament over his slain grandson, Neoptolemos, at the end of Euripides' *Andromache*. Peleus, however, receives consolation from his divine wife, Thetis, appearing as dea ex machina, in contrast to the harshness of Dionysos as deus ex machina here.

There is a further irony in Kadmos' lament: it echoes a heroic pattern in Homeric father-son relationships, for it harks back to Achilles' request for information about his father, Peleus, when he meets Odysseus in Hades (*Odyssey* 11. 494–503):

> Tell me if you have any news of blameless Peleus, whether he still has honor among the Myrmidons, or whether they dishonor him in Hellas and Phthia, because old age holds his hands and feet. If I should come there to my father's house as his helper, up into the rays of the sun, even for a little while, such as I was once in broad Troy when I slew the best of the host, truly would I make hateful to them my strength and my invincible hands, to them who do him violence and deprive him of honor.

Although Kadmos' situation in the *Bakkhai* is that of Achilles' father, Peleus, rather than of the Achilles who speaks these lines in the *Odyssey*, the father-son relationships is still analogous. Kadmos praises Pentheus in the terms that evoke the traditional heroic code of the mighty son who is defending an old, impotent father against enemies who surround him and would "do him violence and deprive him of honor" (cf. "dishonored," 1494, 1502). Like Achilles too, Kadmos combines defencelessness against dishonor with the threat of insult (*hubris*, 1492, cf. Achilles' line about violence and dishonor, *Od.* 11.503). But of course Pentheus and his unheroic death in female dress and at the hands of women are at the furthest possible remove from the heroic spirit of Achilles; and the situation is the reverse of that of the *Odyssey* passage, with the old man, not the son, as the speaker.

1512 The second major lacuna in the text. It probably contained the first part of Dionysos' prophecy. Here too we have provided a restoration on the basis of the *Christus Patiens*; see the Appendix.

1543 *changed to a dragon-snake* This part of Dionysos' prophecy harks back to the mythical origins of Thebes, which Kadmos had founded by slaying the serpent that guarded the spring of Dirké at the site of Thebes. There is, perhaps, a cruel irony in this transformation of Thebes' founder into the form of the monstrous creature that he had defeated in his youth.

1545–46 *Harmonia, Ares' daughter* The marriage of a mortal man and a goddess was a mark of exceptional happiness. Pindar, *Pythian* 3.88–92, cites the bliss of this wedding and that of Peleus and Thetis as the highest felicity for mortals but adds that it is followed by the inevitable sorrows of mortality.

1547–52 *And you and she, as was foretold . . . undergo a journey* Euripides here alludes to traditions, mentioned in Herodotus (*Histories* 5.61 and 9.43), according to which the exiled Kadmos, transformed into a snake, leads a people from Illyria (in the area of northwestern Greece or Albania) known as the Encheleis against Greece, where they will sack Apollo's shrine at Delphi.

1555 *land of the blessèd* Like some other heroes with divine connections (Peleus, Achilles, Menelaus), Kadmos will eventually be transported to Elysium, the land of the blest.

1580–82 *not even after I sail / The River Acheron . . . peace* Kadmos finds no solace in Dionysos' promise of Elysium in 1555. While translation to Elysium usually means avoidance of Hades (so, for instance, for Menelaus in Homer, *Odyssey* 4.561–69), Kadmos seems to assume the normal process of a mortal end. Possibly he thinks that he will go to Hades first and be taken from there to Elysium, but the point of the lines is probably his intense feeling of continuing misery rather than any precise underworld topography. The lines add to the mood of unrelieved sorrow at the end. He has none of the "peace" or "calm" that belongs among the blessings enjoyed by the god and his worshipers (e.g., 460, 720, 740, 906).

1585 *a useless old white swan* The exact point of the swan image has been much discussed. The primary associations are probably of the white hair of old age and the swan's lament at its death.

1592 *to Aristaios* A line has dropped out, and it is unclear exactly where Kadmos is telling Agauë to go. The reference completes the pattern associating Pentheus' suffering with that of his cousin Aktaion.

1598 *Yes, because of us he suffered things / So terrible* The manuscript here reads, "I endured from you terrible things," which would have to be spoken by Dionysos. The attribution of lines to speakers is notoriously unreliable in our manuscripts. Line 1568 looks like Dionysos' exit line, and so we follow most editors in emending 1598 and assigning it to Kadmos. The change in the Greek wording is slight.

1609–13 *Many are the shapes of what's divine* This choral tag closes four other plays (*Alcestis*, *Medea*, *Andromache*, and *Helen*). Though originally written by Euripides, it was not intended for this play and is a later addition.

APPENDIX: RECONSTRUCTION OF THE FRAGMENTARY ENDING

The text of the second half of the *Bakkhai* (from line 866 on) depends on a single surviving manuscript, the fourteenth-century Palatinus (P), which has lost some material near the end of the play. There are two places where there is a jump in the sense that indicates a possible lacuna in the manuscript. The first lacuna comes after 1461, the second after 1512. The text of the first passage is as follows:

> AGAUË   Father—where's the dear body of my
>   child?   1459
>
> KADMOS   I made a long hard search for it; I bring
>   it with me.   1460
>
> AGAUË   Has all of it—the limbs—been placed to-
>   gether decently?   1461
>
>   [. . .]
>
> AGAUË   How much of my madness did Pentheus
>   share with me?   1482

The interruption of the line-by-line question and answer (*stichomythia*) between 1461 and 1482 indicates that something has been lost, but it is still debated whether this gap contained only a few lines or an extensive passage, presumably containing Agauë's lament.

That there exists a substantial lacuna in the second passage, after 1512, is generally agreed, but what it contained obviously depends on the reconstruction of the first passage. In line 1512 Agauë exclaims, "Father! You see how my life is overturned." In the next line of the manuscript text, 1543, Dionysos has already entered and has been prophesying Kadmos' exile and transformation into a serpent. Somewhere in this part of the play Agaue lamented over Pentheus' body. There are two interrelated problems: first, whether Agaue's lament came in the first or second lacuna (that is, after 1461 or after 1512), and, second, whether or not she pieced together Pentheus' torn body on the stage (a scene known as the *Compositio Membrorum*). For reasons that will appear below, I believe that both lacunae are extensive, perhaps fifty to sixty lines in the first and some twenty in the second.

Reconstruction of the missing verses depends on a few remarks and quotations from later ancient authors, on the *Christus Patiens* (*The Passion of Christ*), a twelfth-century Byzantine play about the Passion of Christ once attributed to Gregory the Great, and on a papyrus fragment to be discussed later. The *Christus Patiens* is a cento of verses drawn from the entire corpus of Euripides' plays. It makes heavy use of the *Bakkhai* and includes lines that probably came from the play's lost portions.

Fundamental for the reconstruction of the scene is the remark of the third-century C.E. rhetorician Apsines:

> In Euripides Agaue, mother of Pentheus, having passed beyond her madness and having recognized her own son now torn apart, accuses herself and arouses pity ... In this passage Euripides' wish was to arouse pity for Pentheus, and he has in fact aroused it, for the mother holding each of his limbs in her hands laments over each of them.

Apsines' comment indicates that Agaue not only laments over the body, which is a familiar enough motif in Greek tragedy, but, at the least, handles the mangled parts, which is unexampled in the genre. Some scholars have argued that Agaue merely touches or caresses the limbs and does not actually piece the body together on the stage. Favoring an on-stage *Compositio Membrorum* is the ending of Seneca's *Phaedra* (middle of the first century C.E.), where Theseus recomposes the mangled body of his son, Hippolytus (lines 1247–74). Seneca may be imitating Euripides' scene with Agaue and Pentheus. But it can also be argued that Seneca is elaborating the Euripidean material in a new and characteristically Senecan way. On the negative side too is the omission of this scene from the First Hypothesis of the *Bakkhai*; but this summary of the play contains a number of textual corruptions and is perhaps itself fragmentary toward the end.

If Agaue merely handles or caresses the torn but already recomposed body, Kadmos' reply in the gap after 1461 was something like this: "Yes, the body is all decently put together, for we gathered the bloody parts scattered over the stones and trees and bushes. But you still hold the head in your hands." Agauë, then, amid renewed tears, places the head on the corpse and enters upon her formal lament. If, on the other hand, she does recompose the body, Kadmos would have replied: "No (it is not decently composed), for you and your sisters left the limbs scattered far and wide; but, in so far as we could, we have brought them together; and here are the torn pieces on this bier." Agauë and Kadmos then join in piecing the fragments together. As the final gesture, Agauë would lay in place the head, which she carries.

The difference between the two reconstructions lies ultimately only in the degree of the horror; and it is not surprising that many find the more gruesome second alternative too outrageous even for late Euripides. In either case, if we are to believe Apsines, Euripides has given a sensationally grisly twist to the lament over a brutally torn corpse, as we find it, for example, in Sophocles' *Aias* of around 450 B.C.E. (lines 896–973) or in Euripides' own *Trojan Woman* of 415 B.C.E. (lines 1156–1237), about a decade before the *Bakkhai*. In both of these earlier plays the body is on stage and the physical ugliness of the wounds is much in evidence, but neither body is torn to bits nor requires the handling or adjusting of the parts, as in Agauë's lament. On either reconstruction of Agauë's lament, she would conclude with a final, tearful view of the body as she covers it with a veil or shroud. Kadmos then says something like, "My miserable daughter, I pity you, but such is the cruel madness that Dionysos sent upon you." Agauë responds with line 1482, where our text resumes, "How much of my madness did Pentheus share with me?" She asks this question in her continuing self-accusation, which, as Apsines remarked (see above), accompanied her recomposition of the body. With the deepened understanding that comes in the course of her lament, she shifts from blaming Dionysos, as she does in her moment of recognition in 1457 ("Now I see that Dionysos crushed us") to blaming herself and her "madness" in 1482. In his reply Kadmos explains Pentheus' guilt (1483–84), "He proved himself to be like you — he refused / To revere the gods," whereupon he moves into his own briefer and less violent lamentation (1490–1509).

Taken together, the laments of Agauë and Kadmos, whatever their relative order, complement one another as characteristic modes of female and male mourning in the polis. Agauë is intensely physical, as one would expect from a mother. She handles and touches the torn body, perhaps caresses and kisses it, probably refers to having given birth and nursed Pentheus (see *Christus Patiens* 1256–57, below), and finally covers the corpse with a robe or veil that she carries (*Christus Patiens* 1123, 1470–72, below), much as Tekmessa, for example, covers the body of Aias (Sophocles, *Aias* 915–16) or Hecuba does that of As-tyanax in the *Trojan Women* (1218–20).

A strong argument for placing Agauë's lament before Kadmos' is staging. Her entrance with Pentheus' head is a spectacular *coup de théâtre*, vividly remembered centuries later, as Plutarch's anecdote in his *Life of Crassus* attests (see the Introduction, p. 6); but it is hard to imagine Agauë standing with that head all through the following scene. It is easier to suppose that she placed the head on the body in the lacuna after 1461. In this way Kadmos speaks his lament over a fully recomposed body. For the dramatic rhythm of the play, too, it seems more effective for Agauë's highly emotional lament to precede Kadmos' speech. Kadmos' somewhat calmer lament would then modulate to a less vehement emotional tone and help lead into the speech of Dionysos, with its prophecy of the future.

On this reconstruction Agauë's inquiry about the body and its condition in 1459–61 (cited above) leads naturally into the lament (with or without the *Compositio Membrorum*). Her entrance with Pentheus' head at the beginning of the scene (1356) has alerted the audience to the grisly scene that follows. The line-by-line dialogue of the "psychotherapy scene," in which Kadmos gradually brings Agauë back to sanity and reality, leads inexorably to her readiness to confront the consequences of her actions. First she recognizes the head (1445); then she asks who was the killer and receives the direct reply, despite the pounding of her heart (1449), "You and your sisters were the ones who killed him" (1450). Her exclamation of recognition at 1457, "Now I see that Dionysos crushed us," shows her moral readiness and growing strength for the experience that she must now undergo. When she next asks (1459), "Father— where's the dear body of my child?" she is fully prepared to face this most visible and horrible sign of her madness. Kadmos' response, "I made a long hard search for it; I bring it with me" (1460), can be taken as an implicit stage direction, calling attention to the body that his attendants carried in on the bier. Line 1460, in fact, seems to hark back self-consciously to Kadmos' entrance with the body at 1371.

In his commentary on the *Bakkhai*, E. R. Dodds argues that line 1482, "How much of my madness did Pentheus share with me?" "seems to belong more naturally to an earlier stage, at which Agauë is still trying to get the facts clear" (Dodds on 1300, p. 232). But the line makes equal sense as part of a movement back from the intense emotion of her lament, with its awful physical contact with the body, to an attempt to understand the cruelty of Dionysos' punishment. The line thus helps effect a transition to the more restrained (if still painful) mood first of

Kadmos' lament and then of Dionysos' prophecy. It also shows Euripides continuing to hammer away at the cruelty of the god's revenge, as the two mortal protagonists struggle to understand it and come to terms with it (1456–58, 1482, 1561–67, 1592–99).

New evidence for the missing lines emerged some forty years ago in the form of some small scraps of a papyrus codex from Antinoë (also called Antinoöpolis) in Egypt of the fifth century C.E., one line of which (fragment ii b verso, 4, in Diggle's Oxford Text) seems to confirm that *Christus Patiens* 1471–72 does indeed echo our play: "I cover your blood-spattered limbs, torn in furrows, with my fresh robes" (see p. 93 of the translation, above, after 1461). From the number of lines per page in the codex, Dodds calculated that if there was a major lacuna after 1461 (and not just the omission of two or three lines), then the missing portion of the text would have to be "at least fifty lines long" (p. 244); and so he preferred to place the *Compositio Membrorum* after 1512, on the grounds that a fifty-plus line speech by Agauë after 1461 would be too long. But a fifty-line speech by Agauë after 1461 is by no means impossible.[1] Hecuba's lament over the shattered body of Astyanax at the end of the *Trojan Women* occupies some sixty lines (*Tro.* 1156–1215); and for the *Bakkhai* passage one has to allow also for some preliminary description by Kadmos, dialogue between Kadmos and Agauë, and possible remarks by the chorus. The fragmentary condition of the papyrus codex leaves many uncertainties, and it is by no means sure that all of the papyrus fragments pertain to the *Bakkhai*.[2]

In assigning verses of the *Christus Patiens* to the two lacunae, I have followed Diggle's Oxford Text (pp. 354–55). The words in parentheses are editorial changes from or extrapolations to the *Christus Patiens* to reflect what might have been the Euripidean original.

FRAGMENTS OF LOST PORTIONS OF THE *BAKKHAI*

A. *Lines of the* Christus Patiens *possibly drawn from the* Bakkhai

I. *Assigned to Agauë's lament, after* Bakkhai *1461. (Agauë is the speaker).*

1011 Alas for me, in my wretched misery, I who once was blest with happiness.

1120 These men here do not give heed to how to put you in your tomb. How then

---

1. D. H. Roberts, the editor of the Antinoë fragment, cited by Dodds, drew just the opposite conclusion from the papyrus and preferred to place the *Compositio Membrorum* after 1461.
2. See Diggle's note ad loc. in his Oxford text (p. 352).

shall I (do so)? In what sort of tomb can I place your body? With what sort of robes can I cover your corpse?

1256 How can I (lift) these limbs, kissing that (torn) flesh to which I myself gave birth?

1312 How can I, in my misery, in my caring for you, lift you to my breast? What manner of dirge can I sing?

1449 [Yes, let us bury this body], but it is a small consolation to the dead.

1466 Come then, old man, let us fit the head of this poor child into its proper place, and let us fit together the whole body harmoniously as best we can. O dearest face, o youthful cheek! Look, with this veil I am covering your head, and I am sheltering with my fresh robes your blood-spattered limbs, all rent in furrows.

[Note: The last line seems to coincide with a fragment of the Antinoë papyrus: see above. C. W. Willink, "Some Problems of Text and Interpretation in the Bacchae I," Classical Quarterly 16 (1966), p. 45, with note 5, suggests that the first sentence, 1466–68, was addressed by Kadmos to Agauë, with "old man" displacing an original "poor woman." Line 1449 above would then have followed, also spoken by Kadmos. Lines 1466–68, if derived from the Bakkhai, would seem to imply the piecing together of the body on stage.]

II. Assigned to the lacuna after Kadmos' lament (after Bakkhai 1512).
(DIONYSOS appears, perhaps in a crane above the orchestra, or perhaps on the roof of the stage building, and addresses AGAUË and KADMOS.)

1756 Dionysos addresses Agauë: And you, so eager for murder, must leave the city.
[Note: Another possible translation of this line is "You must leave the city that is so eager for murder." Dionysos' command of Agauë's exile, because she is polluted with the blood of her son, must have come in the missing part of his speech, perhaps before his prophecy of Kadmos' sufferings, as he is still addressing Kadmos where our text resumes at 1543.

The First Hypothesis notes that "Dionysos, when he appeared, announced some things to all, and then made clear to each [of the protagonists] what will happen." Agauë's exclamations to Kadmos at the end also presuppose that she has received this sentence of exile: (1567): "Aiee. It is decided, Father. Exile, misery"; (1583): "O Father, I am exiled deprived of you!" Dionysos' prophecy of Agauë's exile may have come, in part, in reply to her possible accusation of the god after 1329, "Father! You see how my life is overturned," especially if these words are the prelude to her bitter complaint against Dionysos. The continuing anger of his reply might have contained *Christus Patiens* 1756, which seems to indicate his unpitying harshness as he describes Agauë (or possibly "the city") as "eager for murder," "thirsting for slaughter" (*phonôsan*). Sophocles uses this verb in the *Antigone* (117) of the spears of the attackers thirsting for the blood of the citizens. If this verse of the *Christus Patiens* does indeed come from the *Bakkhai*, Dionysos is evoking the pollution that necessitates Agauë's exile from Thebes; and he cruelly reminds her, in her present sorrow, of the horror of her past madness. We may compare Artemis' punitive speech to Theseus at the end of *Hippolytos (Hipp.* 1283–1324).]

300 That you may find out and come to know your deserved punishment.

1690 I shall declare the sufferings that this man here (Kadmos) is going to fulfill.

1360 For (you) brought forth against me unseemly words, falsely claiming that (Semelé) bore me from some mortal man. Nor was this enough for (you) in (your) outrageous insults to me.

1663 Thus was he (Pentheus) killed by those from whom he should least have died, (for) he came to (use) chains (against me) and jeering words.

[Note: *Christus Patiens* seems to have recast Euripides to refer to the victim here (Jesus Christ), but the "chains" of 1663 seem to derive from Pentheus' attempt to imprison the Stranger and the maenads in the first half of the play].

1665 Such things did your people, whom he loved, in (the frenzy of) anger . . . , do to their benefactor. And so he suffered these things not (undeservedly). But the evils that your people must suffer I shall not conceal. You shall leave the city, yielding to barbarians, a slave, an exile from home; for it is prophesied that (you) must traverse every barbarian land, prisoners taken by the spear, enduring many woes [cf. *Bakkhai* 1573–78] . . . For you must leave this city, paying the penalty for your unholy pollution to the one whom (you) killed . . . , and you shall look upon your native land no longer. For it is not holy for the murderers to remain among the tombs of those they have slain. And you shall come to many cities, ill-starred that you are, bearing the yoke of slavery [cf. *Bakkhai* 1548–50].

[Note: The first part of Dionysos' prophecy seems to allude to the exile of Kadmos and his people, driven out of Thebes and forced to join a barbarian tribe known as the Encheleis, usually located on the Illyrian coast though sometimes farther north, with whom they will sack Delphi. The legend is referred to in Herodotus, *Histories* 5.61; see Dodds on 1330–39, pp. 235–36; also above on 1547–52)].

1639 *(Kadmos, replying to Dionysos)* By what (you) have wrought I consider (you) clearly a god.

B. UNPLACED FRAGMENTS (FROM VARIOUS OTHER SOURCES)

1. Cited by scholion to Aristophanes, *Plutus* 907 (= Euripides, fragment 847, in Augustus Nauck, ed., *Tragicorum Graecorum Fragmenta*, 2nd. ed. [Leipzig 1889], possibly from Agauë's lament: For if I had not taken this defilement into my hands . . . [Alternatively: Would that I had not taken this defilement into my hands.]

2. Cited by Lucian, *Piscator* 2, but not specifically attributed to the *Bakkhai* ; possibly from Agauë's lament: To find his doom mangled among the rocks. [Note: These words, which do not form a complete sentence, could have been spoken by Kadmos, early in the lacuna after 1300, explaining to Agauë how Pentheus died].

Antinoë Papyrus 24, fifth century C.E. Fragments of eight lines, among which the following words are intelligible: . . . your blood-spattered limbs, all rent in furrows . . . Know that . . . Let him learn . . . Zeus is the one who . . . And someone (?) . . .

[Note: Sufficient letters of the first line remain to make it likely that this is the same verse as *Christus Patiens* 1471, cited above. But it is not certain how much of the rest of the passage comes from the *Bakkhai*.]

GLOSSARY

ACHERON: river in Epirus in northwestern Greece, supposed to lead to the underworld. Popular etymology connected it with the Greek word *akhos* (woe) as the "river of sorrow."

AGAUË: daughter of Kadmos and mother of Pentheus by the Planted Man, Ekhion (q.v.); leader of the Theban women whom Dionysos has punished by madness and driven to Mount Kithairon. Some translators latinize this name to Agave.

AGENOR: king of Sidon in Phoenicia and father of Kadmos.

AKHELOÜS: the largest river of Greece, located in the northwest and forming the border between Aetolia and Acarnania. It is often regarded as the father of the fresh-water springs of Greece, as here of the Theban spring Dirké.

AKTAION: son of Autonoë and so cousin of Pentheus; his death is closely parallel to that of Pentheus—he offends the goddess Artemis and is punished in the wild (in the same place as Pentheus) by being torn apart by his hounds. In some versions of the myth Artemis turns him into a stag.

APHRODITE: goddess of love, worshiped in a famous sanctuary on Cyprus.

APOLLO: brother of Artemis, god of prophecy, healing, archery. Particularly important is his oracular shrine at Delphi on Mount Parnassus, where Dionysos is said to spend the winter months while Apollo is absent in the mythical paradise of the Hyperboreans.

ARES: god of war; here father of Harmonia, the wife of Kadmos.

ARISTAIOS: father of Aktaion (q.v.) and husband of Autonoë, Agaue's sister. Elsewhere he appears as a minor divinity of hunting, herding, and bee-keeping.

ARTEMIS: sister of Apollo; goddess of the hunt, often represented as dancing or hunting in the company of forest nymphs in wild places, where Aktaion (q.v.) has his fatal encounter with her.

ASOPOS: river that flows through the central plain of Boeotia, near Thebes; also personified as a river god, father of various nymphs of the region.

AUTONOË: daughter of Kadmos and sister of Agaue.

AXIOS: River of Macedonia, now the Vadar.

BAKKHAI: women worshipers in the cult of Dionysos; the word derives from one of the several names of the god, Bakkhos. Sometimes latinized as Bacchantes or Bacchants.

BAKKHOS: another name for Dionysos, especially in connection with his ecstatic rites.

BAKTRIA: a mountainous area of central Asia, in the region of modern Afghanistan.

BROMIOS: an epithet of Dionysos, as "Roarer," perhaps because of his associations with the bull, the lion, and earthquakes, or because of his birth from lightning, or because of the noise that accompanies his rites.

CRETE: large island south of mainland Greece; in myth the birthplace of Zeus, sheltered from Kronos by his mother Rhea in a cave on Mount Dikté, in the eastern part of the island.

CYPRUS: island in the southeastern Mediterranean closely associated with Aphrodite, who is often called Kypris, "the Cyprian one."

DELPHI: Site of a celebrated sanctuary of Apollo on Mount Parnassus (q.v.) in north-central Greece, seat of the most important oracle of the Greeks, and place of the Pythian games, held every four years. It was thought that Dionysos sojourned there in the winter months, during Apollo's absence. The twin peaks above the sanctuary, known as the Phaidriades, "the shining (rocks)," are often mentioned by classical authors as a place of Dionysos' epiphany; and the upland plateau near these rocks are also a locale of the Bakkhantes' nocturnal torchlight processions, the *oreibasia* or "walk on the mountain."

DEMETER: goddess of the fruitful earth, the harvest, and fertility, closely associated with the young god Iakkhos, identified with Dionysos, in her mystery cult at Eleusis, near Athens.

DESIRE: a handsome youth, the personification of sexual longing (Pothos in Greek), who often appears in Dionysiac scenes on vases and is associated with the sensual aspect of the god.

DIRKÉ: a famous spring at Thebes where Kadmos killed a huge serpent guarding the water, thereby founding the city.

DIONYSOS: also referred to as Bakkhos, Bromios, Euios, and Iakkhos; god of wine and intoxication, but also of fertilizing liquids and of civic festive license. Son of Zeus and the mortal Theban princess, Semelé (q.v.), sister of Agauë; hence he is the cousin of Pentheus. Born at Thebes after Semelé's death from Zeus' lightning, he is kept safe in Zeus' thigh until his second birth from his divine father. Though established very early in Greece, he is imagined as a new arrival whose cult often meets resistance or hostility, which he overcomes by the violent punishment of his opponents. His worship has special (though not exclusive) appeal to women and takes the form, in part, of ecstatic rites of song, dance, and excited processions outside the city, including the hunting down and tearing apart of wild animals (the *sparagmos* or ritual rending). He appears to his worshipers in epiphanies marked by bright light and thunderous noise and in the form of a bull, lion, or snake.

DITHYRAMBOS: A cult title of Dionysos, sometimes derived from the Greek words *dis* (twice) and *thura* (door, i.e., he who came twice to the doors" [of birth] in his second birth from Zeus's thigh). As a common noun, the word refers to an excited choral song in honor of Dionysos.

EKHION: father of Pentheus; one of the Planted Men, sprung from the teeth of the serpent slain by Kadmos to found Thebes (q.v.).

ELEKTRAN GATE: one of the seven gates of Thebes.

EROTES: small gods of love and desire, the "Loves," we might say; the word is the plural of the name of the god of sexual desire, Eros.

ERYTHRAI: town on the slopes of Mount Kithairon attacked by the Bakkhai in the play.

EUHOI!:   The usual cry of the participants in the Dionysiac rites, expressing intense excitement and abandon.

EUIOS: epithet of Dionysos, derived from the ecstatic cry *"Euhoi"*; "he whom one celebrates with the cry of Euhoi."

FURY (in Greek, Lyssa):   personified divinity of madness, often represented as resembling one of the dread Furies (Erinyes) of the underworld.

GIANTS: a mythical older race of beings who challenge the gods and are defeated by them in battle.

GORGONS, LIBYAN: three monstrous sisters, of whom the best known is the snaky-haired Medusa. They are descended from primordial sea divinities and dwell in the remote West, far from civilized humanity. The epithet "Libyan" also enhances the sense of strangeness and monstrosity.

GRACES: beautiful young goddesses, usually three in number. They personify physical and artistic beauty. Associated with Aphrodite as well as Dionysos, they are bringers of the charm and delight of song, dance, and poetry. They have connections with sexuality, fertility, and birth in addition to poetry and art.

HADES: the underworld, imagined as a grim and shadowy place for the lifeless shades after death; also personified as the god of the underworld, sharing the world with his brothers, Zeus, god of the sky, and Poseidon, lord of the sea.

HERA: daughter of Kronos and Rhea, sister and wife of Zeus, noted for her jealousy of Zeus' amours and her hostility to the off-spring of these unions. In the mythical background to the *Bakkhai* she tricks Semelé into a fiery death from Zeus' lightning.

HYSIAI: town on the slopes of Mount Kitháiron attacked by the Bakkhai in the play.

IAKKHOS: a youthful divinity, closely associated with Demeter as the divine child; he has an important place in her mystery cult at Eleusis. Though originally distinct from Dionysos, he gradually becomes identified with him. His name may originally have meant "Lord of the shouting," derived from the "shouting" (in Greek *iakkhein*) that attended the processions and rites at Eleusis.

INO: sister of Agauë, the mother of Pentheus and daughter of Kadmos. Elsewhere in myth she is driven mad by Hera and leaps into the sea with her infant son, Melikertes, whereupon both are changed into minor sea divinities.

IO!:   exclamation of joy or fear or sorrow, like our "Oh!"

ISMENOS: a stream that flows through the city of Thebes.

KADMOS: Son of Agenor, king of Sidon in Phoenicia; father of Agauë and Semelé; aged patriarch of the ruling house of Thebes, which he founds by slaying the serpent at its spring, Dirké (q.v.). Having no sons, he has given his rule to his grandson, Pentheus.

KITHÁIRON: mountain near Thebes and the site of the Dionysiac rites of the Theban women who are driven mad by the god and so made maenads (q.v.).

KORYBANTËS: a band of young men who worship the Phrygian mother-goddess Kybelé (q.v.) in ecstatic and noisy rites; hence their association with Dionysos.

KORYKIAN MOUNTAIN PEAKS: a sacred area high on Mount Parnassus noted especially for the cave of the Korykian Nymphs, whose worship is associated with that of Dionysos. The latinized form is Corycian.

KOURÉTES: a band of young men closely associated with the goddess Rhea, mother of Zeus. They helped protect the infant Zeus from his murderous father, Kronos, by drowning out his cries with their noisy music. They are sometimes identified with the Korybantës (q.v.) and are associated with male rites of passage to adolescence.

KRONOS: ruler of the gods in the generation before the Olympians, husband of Rhea and father of Zeus and Hera. Fearful of a son who would overthrow him, he swallowed all his offspring at birth, except Zeus, who was hidden and saved by his mother. Having grown to manhood, Zeus overthrew Kronos and then established the pantheon of the Greek gods.

KYBELÉ: Phrygian mother goddess, sometimes called "mountain mother of the gods" and also identified with Rhea, mother of Zeus and Hera. Her worship on mountains and in processions of ecstatic followers was accompanied by the wild music of flutes, drums, and cymbals and so was felt to be akin to the riotous aspects of Dionysiac cult. The more familiar Latin form is Cybele.

LYDIA: Country in western Asia Minor famous for its wealth, luxury, and sensuality; regarded as the origin of Dionysos' cult.

LYDIAS: river of Macedonia, now the Mavronero.

MAENADS: female devotees of Dionysos in their excited, ecstatic state. The word in Greek means mad women, women who are raving or frantic, and so it has pejorative connotations. In the play it generally refers to the Theban women driven mad by Dionysos. The more neutral term for such women is "bakkhai" (q.v.), though this too can have associations of violent emotion.

MEDES: ancient inhabitants of what is now Iran.

MUSES: young female goddesses of music, song, and dance; born on Pieria on the northern slopes of Olympus; traditionally regarded as the nine daughters of Zeus and Mnemosyné (Memory).

NYSA: a mountain sacred to Dionysos located in different areas, particularly Egypt, Italy, Asia Minor, and Thrace.

OLYMPOS: a mountain, in northeastern Greece, the peak of which is the home of the Greek gods, who are therefore often called the Olympians; the area is also associated with Dionysos and his worship.

ORPHEUS: a mythical singer of northeastern Greece, sometimes regarded as the son of Apollo and the Muse Calliope. His power of song was so compelling that even the beasts and the forests followed him as he sang. He is closely associated with Dionysos and is regarded as the mythical founder of the Dionysiac mysteries.

PAN: god of forests and mountains, particularly Arcadia in the mountainous area of the south-central Peloponnesos. Son of Hermes and a forest nymph, he is closely associated with shepherds and herding. He is usually represented as grotesquely half-human and half-goat, playing the flute and joining the forest nymphs in dances in wild and deserted places.

PAPHOS: Site of a famous sanctuary of Aphrodite on Cyprus, q.v.

PARNASSOS: Mountain to the west of Thebes, the site of Delphi, an important oracular shrine of Apollo, and also closely associated with Dionysos, who comes during the winter months, when Apollo is absent. It is one of the places of ritual processions by the Bakkhai.

PENTHEUS: son of Agaué, grandson of Kadmos, who has handed on to him the rule of Thebes (q.v.); his father, absent from the play, is Ekhion, one of the Planted Men (q.v.). He is Dionysos' antagonist in the *Bakkhai*.

PHRYGIA: an area in northwestern Anatolia, home of the goddess Kybelé, (q.v.).

PIERIA: A mountainous area in northeastern Greece, along the slopes of Olympus, traditionally the birthplace of the Muses and so associated with song and poetry.

PLANTED MEN: warriors who sprang from the teeth of the serpent that Kadmos killed at the Theban spring of Dirké; they then become the future population of Thebes. Hence the Thebans are often called *Spartoi* (Sown Men or Planted Men).

RHEA: ancient goddess, wife of Kronos and mother of Zeus, sometimes identified with Kybelé.

SARDIS: major city of Lydia, famous for its wealth and luxury.

SATYRS: animalistic followers of Dionysos, with human bodies but horses' ears, tails, and hooves; represented in myth and in vase-painting as drunken and lecherous.

SEMELÉ: Kadmos' daughter and sister of Agauë, Ino, and Autonoé. Beloved by Zeus, she is tricked by Hera into asking her divine lover to appear to her in his full celestial splendor. Blasted by Zeus' lightning, she gives fiery birth to Dionysos (q.v.), whom Zeus then preserves in his thigh until he is ready for his final birth. She is honored at Thebes by a shrine from which smoke from Zeus' lightning still rises. Semelé probably has her origins in a Phrygian earth- and fertility-goddess, Semelô.

SIDON: city in Phoenicia, ruled over by Agénor, father of Kadmos, and the original home of Kadmos.

TEIRESIAS: blind prophet of Thebes; he has an important role in other Theban myths and in other Greek tragedies set in Thebes, like Sophocles' *Antigone* and *Oedipus Tyrannos*.

THEBES: ancient city in Boeotia in Greece; settled by Kadmos after his victory over a serpent that guarded its spring, Dirké (q.v.). Kadmos populated the city with the Planted Men (q.v.), sprung from the teeth of the serpent that he sowed or "planted" in the earth. Presently ruled over by Pentheus, grandson of Kadmos and son of the Planted Man, Ekhion. Birthplace of Dionysos. Famous for its walls and seven gates. It is the subject of a number of early epic poems dealing with struggles for its throne after the death of Oedipus, and it is the setting for many tragedies about Oedipus and his children.

THIASOS: A holy band of men or women, joined together by their worship of a divinity. Here it refers to the band of women, whether from Lydia or in Thebes, who follow Dionysos and are inspired by his ecstatic rites. Plural is *thiasoi*.

THYRSOS: long fennel-stalk (in itself called the narthex), tipped with ivy leaves, carried by Bakkhai in their excited dances. Plural is *thyrsoi*.

TMOLOS: Mountain in Lydia, celebrated for its gold.

ZEUS: ruler of the gods on Olympus, son of Kronos (q.v.), husband of Hera, and father of Dionysos by the mortal Theban princess, Semelé. Originally a sky god, associated particularly with lightning and other celestial phenomena.

CPSIA information can be obtained at www.ICGtesting.com
Printed in the USA
BVOW02s1149120814

362533BV00001B/1/A